Contents

Foreword

I've known Jimmy since he was very young. I saw him be a decent husband and father in his first marriage and very successful in his business career. Following the end of that marriage, I saw him quickly hit a hell of insanity and depravity as a result of his drug addiction and alcoholism. As a result of his spiritual 12-step program and his dedicated study of *A Course in Miracles*, he has become an inspiration to many others. He's even been taking more of my suggestions!

In late September of 2016, Jimmy felt he was ready to start this book. I suggested to him that he read through *A Course in Miracles* one more time before beginning his book. He took my suggestion and, over the next 3 months, he read through the 3 books of *A Course in Miracles,* the <u>Text</u>, the <u>Workbook for Students</u> and the <u>Manual for Teachers</u>. He also read once again the two short supplements contained in his copy of *A Course in Miracles - Psychotherapy: Purpose, Process and Practice* and *The Song of Prayer – Prayer, Forgiveness, Healing.*

I have reviewed this book and it certainly contains some valuable insight into *A Course in* Miracles. Jimmy's book is intended primarily for individuals who have been through the 3 books of *A Course in Miracles* at least once. *Course* students who have a reasonable understanding of the mind training purpose of the *Course* will generally enjoy and benefit from this book. Although others may read this book and thereby be encouraged to study *A Course in Miracles,* there will be much in this book which makes little or no sense to them.

Jimmy first started studying *A Course in Miracles* in early 1999 and has been a very diligent student since that time. As other students know, the <u>Workbook for Students</u> contains 365 lessons and requires at least one year to complete because students are instructed not to do more than one lesson per day. Jimmy has done these lessons 14 times over the past 18 years. In addition, he has studied the <u>Text</u> and the <u>Manual for Teachers</u> more than 14 times. In recent years, he always studies the two supplements when he studies the other materials.

I know it is Jimmy's intent to continue studying these books for the rest of his earthly life because he continues to get a better understanding and a deeper level of peace and happiness every time he does *A Course in Miracles.*

Again I'll say that this book can be a good tool to other *Course* students and help advance their understanding of the *Course's* thought system.

Jimmy's spiritual advisor

Authors Introduction and Acknowledgements

In order to study *A Course in Miracles* (*ACIM* or the *Course*) one must study *ACIM*. This book is certainly not a substitute for this requirement. However, if you are a *Course* student, this book can be a valuable aid to enhancing your understanding of the *Course* and will encourage some of you to be a more dedicated student.

Part III of this book entitled "me" is a relatively short autobiography of my life. When you read this, you will see that I have a long history of mental illness, drug addiction and alcoholism. If someone like me can become a dedicated student of *ACIM* and year after year become ever happier as a result of its teachings, then I would say that just about anyone else can do the same.

Part I, entitled *"A Course in Miracles"*, is primarily a summary of 5 important topics contained in its pages – (1) The author of the *Course*, (2) Forgiveness, (3) Oneness, (4) Listen to the Voice for God, and (5) Spiritual progress. These are contained in chapters 2 through 6. Chapter 1 is a simple 2-page summary of the major *Course* ideas which can be easily understood by someone who knows nothing about the *Course*. Chapter 7 reproduces my daily long meditation which, by itself, summarizes all the important *Course* ideas.

Part II, entitled Ken Wapnick, includes 43 personal letters Ken and I shared over the last two years of his working live as well as a summary of notes I took while listening on CDs to one of his workshops he gave many years ago. I hope you enjoy the letters as much as I enjoyed receiving Ken's letters to me and writing back to him. You should find a lot of humor intermixed with some solid spirituality.

With respect to ACIM, I must acknowledge the two men who have helped me the most. I had been studying the *Course* for a number of years when it was suggested I read Gary Renard's first book, *The Disappearance of the Universe*. For me, this book advanced my understanding of the *Course* enormously and led me to spending two weekend workshops with Gary as well as going to a spiritual conference in Florida where Gary was one of the speakers. I have also read Gary's other two books and am looking forward to his next one.

Of course, the other man I must acknowledge is Ken Wapnick, who is not only the most recognized *Course* teacher in the world, but also became one of my best friends and my personal spiritual advisor up until his passing in 2013.

Although Ken has passed from this world, his teachings live on in the form of the many *Course* books he wrote, the many workshops he gave, some videos, and the many articles he wrote. Most, perhaps all, of these are available from the "Foundation for *A Course in Miracles*" in Temecula, California. I know I'm not alone when I say to Ken: "I love you my wonderful friend. Much of you lives on in me and continues to help me help others. I'm not exactly sure how it works when we leave this world but I'll just say I'm really looking forward to seeing you again when I get there …. Love Jimmy 'the hat.'"

In 2011, I included in a letter to Ken the following: "Trust me when I say I am thrilled (!) that perhaps the leading emissary of Jesus since Jesus' departure, namely Ken Wapnick, is having personal correspondence with me, Jimmy 'the hat.'" Now, six years later, I'm more convinced than ever that Ken and his work, which lives on, is an incredible communicator of Jesus' teachings from Jesus' wonderful training manual known as *A Course in Miracles*. Based on my experience, I urge other *Course* students to make use of the vast library of teachings Ken left behind which I summarized in the previous paragraph.

I must also thank my wonderful wife Tesha and our two children, Jimesha, age 9 and Jimmy Jr., age 3. Finally, I want to thank my two adult children from my first marriage, Kim and Derek, for their ongoing love and support.

About the Author

Part III of this book contains a good history of Jimmy's life. He came from a solid American family but ended up taking a nose dive into hell due to drugs and alcohol exacerbated by a mental illness. However, as a result of a 12-step spiritual program combined with *A Course in* Miracles, he has risen to a wonderful man with a wonderful life.

Today, Jimmy lives in Southwest Florida with his wife, Tesha, their two children, Jimesha (age 9) and Jimmy Jr. (age 3), and Ollie their dachshund dog. They are a very happy family group living in a very friendly neighborhood.

Jimmy's time today includes a lot of volunteer 12-step work, studying *A Course in Miracles*, valued family time which often means a trip to Disneyworld and the regular business of maintaining the family's home and two vehicles.

If you would like to contact Jimmy personally you can do so by sending an email to:

jimmythehatlaws@aol.com

ACIM Reference System

Naturally within this book I often include quotes from *A Course in Miracles*. I also sometimes include my own comments within these quotes. My comments are always contained within a set of brackets; i.e., [my comments].

The quotations from *A Course in Miracles* are from the combined volume (third edition) copyrighted 2007 by the Foundation for *A Course in Miracles*. They are referenced by the following system:

P – Preface

T- Text

W – Workbook for Students

M – Manual for Teachers (not including Clarification of Terms)

C – Clarification of Terms (last part of Manual for Teachers)

Psy – *Psychotherapy: Purpose, Process and Practice* (24 page supplement to the Course)

Song – *The Song of Prayer* (22 page supplement to the Course)

Examples of this referencing system follow:

"Nothing real can be threatened." (T-Intro.2:2)
Text, Introduction (1st page of the Text), paragraph 2, sentence 2.

"The 'chosen ones' are merely those who choose right sooner." (T-3.IV.7:14)
Text, Chapter 3, Section IV, paragraph 7, sentence 14.

"The world I see offers nothing that I want." (W-128.title)
Workbook for Students, Lesson 128, the title of the lesson.

"There is no world! This is the central thought the course attempts to teach." (W-132.6:2-3)
Workbook for Students, Lesson 132, paragraph 6, sentences 2 and 3.

"God's Son is crucified until you walk along the road with me [Jesus]." (W-Review V.Intro.6:6)
Workbook for Students, Review V, Introduction, paragraph 6, sentence 6.

Note: Part I of the Workbook for Students contains 6 sets of Review lessons which review lessons previously studied. Each of these reviews begins with an Introduction section of one or more pages. These Introduction sections can be found by referencing the following list:

Review I – Immediately following Workbook Lesson 50.
Review II – Immediately following Workbook Lesson 80.
Review III – Immediately following Workbook Lesson 110.
Review IV – Immediately following Workbook Lesson 140.
Review V – Immediately following Workbook Lesson 170.
Review VI – Immediately following Workbook Lesson 200.

"Forgiveness recognizes what you thought your brother did to you has not occurred." (W-Q 1.1:1)
Workbook for Students, Question 1, paragraph 1, sentence 1.

Note: Part II of the Workbook for Students includes 14 important questions and answers. These 14 questions and answers can be found by referencing the following list:

1. What Is Forgiveness? Located after Lesson 220.
2. What Is Salvation? Located after Lesson 230.
3. What Is the World? Located after Lesson 240.
4. What Is Sin? Located after Lesson 250.
5. What Is the Body? Located after Lesson 260.
6. What Is the Christ? Located after Lesson 270.
7. What Is the Holy Spirit? Located after Lesson 280.
8. What Is the Real World? Located after Lesson 290.
9. What Is the Second Coming? Located after Lesson 300.
10. What Is the Last Judgment? Located after Lesson 310.
11. What Is Creation? Located after Lesson 320.
12. What Is the Ego? Located after Lesson 330.
13. What Is a Miracle? Located after Lesson 340.
14. What Am I? Located after Lesson 350.

"It is His [the Holy Spirit's] way that everyone must travel in the end, because it is this ending God Himself appointed." (W-Final Lessons.Intro.2:2)
Workbook for Students, Final Lessons text (found after Lesson 360), Introduction, paragraph 2, sentence 2.

"Prayer now must be the means by which God's Son leaves separate goals and separate interests by, and turns in holy gladness to the truth of union in his Father and himself." (Song-1.Intro.2:4)

The Song of Prayer, Chapter 1, Introduction, paragraph 2, sentence 4.

Part I: A Course in Miracles

Introduction

A Course in Miracles (the *Course*) is not for everyone. Although Jesus tells us this explicitly in his *Course*, I didn't catch on until Ken Wapnick pointed this out to us at a workshop I attended in 2011 or 2012. Here's what Jesus tells us explicitly in the Manual for Teachers: "This is a manual for a special curriculum, intended for teachers of a special form of the universal course [i.e., *A Course in Miracles*]. There are many thousands of other forms, all with the same outcome [waking up in Heaven]." (M-1.4:1-2)

Here's another mistake I made for a while. At one point I had printed off the unedited version of the *Course*, called the URTEXT, and studied it a lot and thought I was becoming the best *Course* student in the world. (I smile at this today.) Again, at a Ken Wapnick workshop, Ken pointed out that the published version is the one we should all be working with. I realize now that in the editing process, Jesus was right there, especially with Helen Schucman, to make sure the published version was what he wanted.

Although I personally have not attempted combining the *Course* with other spiritual philosophies, it has been mentioned by both Ken Wapnick and Gary Renard (and likely by many others) that this is a mistake made by some. If you're doing the *Course*, do only the *Course*! To try and mix the *Course* with other spiritual or religious studies will cause confusion and only cause you delay in reaching your final destination (Heaven).

Here, in Part I of this book, there are 7 chapters. Following is a brief description of each:

> Chapter 1: Summary of *A Course in Miracles* – This is a 2-page summary of the *Course*. It contains the key ideas contained in the *Course* and can be understood by many individuals who know nothing about the *Course*.

> Chapter 2: Jesus is the Author of *A Course in Miracles* – After a brief introductory section, Section B in this chapter identifies a number of

places in the *Course* where Jesus specifically identifies himself as the author. Section C includes many quotes from him especially regarding his availability to us all the time. He is with us always.

Chapter 3: Forgiveness – Again there is a brief introductory section. Section B defines, in my own words, the *Course's* unique definition of forgiveness and shares my personal experience since I've been studying the *Course*. Section C summarizes the importance of forgiveness and simplifies some other *Course* terms which all have the same meaning as forgiveness. Section D offers some of the many specific references to forgiveness contained throughout the *Course*.

Chapter 4: We are all one with our Father – Section A is another summary of the principle ideas contained in the *Course* but with more *Course* terminology. The simplicity of our eternal joyous being is that "We" all share the same single Mind forever and ever. This "We" includes God the Father, the Holy Spirit, all people, animals, fish, plants, things…etc. Section B of this chapter includes some of the many *Course* references to this Oneness which is also called Heaven.

Chapter 5: Listen to Jesus and not to the ego – Section A of this chapter is an overview of this important *Course* goal. Section B includes some of the many references in the *Course* where Jesus tells us of this important idea.

Chapter 6: Spiritual progress – Nobody can go from the world's thought system to God's thought system overnight. Jesus tells us that the Holy Spirit guides us along as we prepare ourselves. I have defined this evolutionary process as spiritual progress. Section A of this chapter talks of this idea and shares some of my experience in this regard over the many years I've been studying the *Course*. Section B includes some of the many *Course* references to this process.

Chapter 7: My long memorized meditation – The meditation contained here is one I do at least once every day. I have found it to be an extremely valuable tool for me. Section A of this chapter offers some insight into this personal habit and Section B includes this meditation as it stands today. If you take a look at it, you might note that it includes all of the major *Course* ideas.

Chapter 1: Summary of *A Course in Miracles*

The purpose of this brief 2-page summary is to give everyone, including those who know nothing about *A Course in Miracles* (the *Course*), an understanding of the major ideas contained in the *Course*. With two exceptions the terminology in this summary is the same as in the *Course*. These exceptions are that instead of the term "God's Son", I have used "God's Child" and instead of the term "sons", I have used "children."

In the beginning, there was only God. God was (and still is) pure Love, never changing but always extending (or always expanding). God, or Love, was full of peace, light, joy, happiness, laughter, freedom and gratitude. He was also forever, or eternal. God, or Love, was also Heaven and this was all there was. There was nothing physical in the entire universe because the entire universe was God or Heaven and pure Spirit.

After some long period of time, God decided He wanted to share Himself with another so He created a Child. This Child is also known as God's Creation. Now everything that God had was given to His Child and everything His Child had was also given to God. They shared the same Mind and there was literally no distinction between the Father and His Child, or God and His Creation. So now Heaven, or Love, consisted of the Father and His Child and everything was wonderful for a long, long time. The only difference between the Father and His Child was that the Father had created the Child and the Child, clearly, had not created the Father. In other words, the Father was the Source and the Child was the Effect. This distinction, however, was never given any thought because the Father and His Child shared the same wonderful Mind, as I stated above. So both God and His Child were full of peace, light, joy, happiness, laughter, freedom and gratitude forever and ever, life without end.

After some time, the Child came up with a crazy idea which was basically "Hey, I'll separate from Dad and go off on my own." The fact is that the Child could not separate from his Father because the Father had created them one. However, the Child could believe that he could separate from his Father which caused the Child to go into a deep coma (or sleep) and started this incredible dream where He believed he had actually separated from His Father.

God, seeing what had happened, immediately created another Entity, Who is referred to as the Holy Spirit, to go into the dream that the Child had made up and wake the Child. I like to think of the Holy Spirit as the Great Divine Psychiatrist. So now Heaven consists of the Father, His Creation (i.e., His Child) and the Holy Spirit.

In the dream that the Child ended up making up, there was this incredible physical world called planet earth along with the sun and moon, other planets, and stars as far as his eyes could see. The dream was exactly opposite to the truth of Heaven. Nothing was eternal. Instead of eternal life, there was death. Instead of absolute oneness, everything was separated from everything else. Instead of pure joy, there was much pain and suffering, intermixed with periods of happy times. Eventually, instead of one Child, totally at one with God, there are now 7.5 billion children each separate from each other and virtually all of them believing they are separate from God Who had created them. Love was replaced with fear.

As I said, God sent the Holy Spirit, the Great Divine Psychiatrist, into the dream to wake up His Child. Although God's Child fell asleep as one while in Heaven, we return individually. The first individual to wake up from the dream was a man we now know as Jesus. Jesus was able to mentally learn from the Holy Spirit and at some point, prior to his execution on the cross, he only listened to the Voice of the Holy Spirit and never adhered to the world's voice (referred to as the ego) which should be considered the voice of insanity.

The job of the Holy Spirit is to wake up all of the children of God and eventually this will in fact happen, although it will likely take millions of years before this occurs. Once the last of us wakes up from our worldly dreams, the physical world and the world of time will just disappear and we'll all be back home in Heaven where we began before we started with our insane idea that we wanted to be separate from our Father.

Chapter 2: Jesus is the Author of *A Course in Miracles*

This chapter consists of 3 sections as follows:

Section A: Introduction

Helen Schucman was the secretary of *A Course in Miracles*. The words that she wrote were given to her by Jesus. In the preface to the *Course*, Helen wrote "Although I had grown more accustomed to the unexpected by that time, I was still very surprised when I wrote, 'This is a course in miracles.' That was my introduction to the Voice. It made no sound, but seemed to be giving me a kind of rapid, inner dictation which I took down in a shorthand notebook." (P-p.viii.beginning with the 2nd line) That Voice that Helen mentally heard was the voice of Jesus.

Section B: Specific references to Jesus authorship

Jesus is the author of *A Course in Miracles*. He tells us this many times throughout this incredible book.

Following are a number of examples where Jesus makes specific reference to himself:

"You are not asked to be crucified, which was part of my own teaching contribution." (T-6.I.6:6)

"My brothers slept during the so-called 'agony in the garden,' but I could not be angry with them because I knew I could not be abandoned." (T-6.I.7:6)

"I elected, for your sake and mine, to demonstrate that the most outrageous assault, as judged by the ego, does not matter. As the world judges these things, but not as God knows them, I was betrayed, abandoned, beaten, torn, and finally killed. It was clear that this was only because of the projection of others onto me, since I had not harmed anyone and had healed many." (T-6.I.9:1-3)

"If the apostles had not felt guilty, they never could have quoted me as saying, 'I come not to bring peace but a sword.' This is clearly the opposite of everything I taught. Nor could they have described my reactions to Judas as they did, if they had really understood me. I could not have said, 'Betrayest thou the Son of man with a kiss?' unless I believed in betrayal. The whole message of the crucifixion was simply that I did not. The 'punishment' I was said to have called forth upon Judas was a similar mistake. Judas was my brother and a Son of God, as much a part of the Sonship as myself. Was it likely that I would condemn him when I was ready to demonstrate that condemnation is impossible?" (T-6.I.15:2-9)

"When I said 'I am with you always,' I meant it literally. I am not absent to anyone in any situation. Because I am always with you, *you* are the way, the truth and the life. You did not make this power, any more than I did. It was created to be shared, and therefore cannot be meaningfully perceived as belonging to anyone at the expense of another. Such a perception makes it meaningless by eliminating or overlooking its real and only meaning." (T-7.III.1:7-12)

"I once asked you to sell all you have and give to the poor and follow me. This is what I meant: If you have no investment in anything in this world, you can teach the poor where their treasure is. The poor are merely those who have invested wrongly, and they are poor indeed! Because they are in need it is given you to help them since you are among them. Consider how perfectly your lesson would be learned if you were unwilling to share their poverty. For poverty is lack, and there is but one lack since there is but one need." (T-12.III.1:1-6) Clearly, someone who is extremely rich financially can be extremely poor by this definition and someone who is extremely poor financially can be extremely rich by this definition.

Section C: More on Jesus and his availability to us

Many students when they first start studying the *Course* have no clue that Jesus authored this wonderful study guide and this was true for me. While it has been many years since my first reading of the *Course*, I'm quite certain that before I finished that first study of its 3 books (Text, Workbook for Students and Manual for Teachers), I was convinced that Jesus was in fact the author.

Over the past 18 years I have studied all 3 books many times over. My own experience has been that each time I study the *Course* is like I'm studying it for the first time. What has been obviously happening for me is that more spiritual nuggets are being discovered as my understanding increases which is a direct result of my ongoing study.

Once we know Jesus is the author, the importance of Jesus to our own salvation and the salvation of the world really comes alive. Following are some of the things he says about himself and what he will do for us:

"I inspire all miracles, which are really intercessions." (T-1.I.32:1)

"Equals should not be in awe of one another because awe implies inequality. It is therefore an inappropriate reaction to me." (T-1.II.3:5-6) Jesus tells us that he is equal to everyone else. His importance lies in the fact that he was the first person to achieve salvation. However, as he clearly tells us in his *Course*, everyone else will accomplish this in their own time until we've all returned to our eternal and timeless Home in Heaven.

"'No man cometh unto the Father but by me' does not mean that I am in any way separate or different from you except in time, and time does not really exist. The statement is more meaningful in terms of a vertical rather than a horizontal axis. You stand below me and I stand below God. In the process of 'rising up,' I am higher because without me the distance between God and man would be too great for you to encompass. I bridge the distance as an elder brother to you on the one hand, and as a Son of God on the other. My devotion to my brothers has placed me in charge of the Sonship, which I render complete because I share it. This may appear to contradict the statement 'I and my Father are one,' but there are two parts to the statement in recognition that the Father is greater." (T-1.II.4:1-7)

"I was a man who remembered spirit and its knowledge. As a man I did not attempt to counteract error with knowledge but to correct error from the bottom up. I demonstrated both the powerlessness of the body and the power of the mind. By uniting my will with that of my Creator, I naturally remembered spirit and its real purpose. I cannot unite your will with God's for you, but I can erase all misperceptions from your mind if you will bring it under my guidance [and remove it from the ego's guidance]. Only your misperceptions stand in your way. Without them your choice is certain. Sane perception induces sane choosing. I cannot choose for you, but I can help you make your own right choice." (T-3.IV.7:3-11)

"I have also made it clear that the resurrection was the means for the return to knowledge [i.e., the return to Heaven], which was accomplished by the union of my will with the Father's." (T-3.V.1:3)

"If you are willing to renounce the role of guardian of your thought system and open it to me, I will correct it very gently and lead you back to God." (T-4.I.4:7)

"I can be entrusted with your body and your ego only because this enables you not to be concerned with them, and lets me teach you their unimportance. I could not understand their importance to you if I had not once been tempted to believe in them myself. [Jesus, like everyone else, believed this world was real before the Voice for God, the Holy Spirit, became his internal guide.] Let us undertake to learn this lesson together so we can be free of them together. I need devoted teachers who share my aim of healing the mind. Spirit is far beyond the need of your protection or mine. Remember this:

> In this world you need not have tribulation because I [Jesus] have overcome the world. That is why you should be of good cheer." (T-4.I.13:4-11) Because Jesus is always with us and always willing to help us if we turn to him, we too can overcome the world and return to Heaven. Clearly, this is wonderful news!

"I have said already that I can reach up and bring the Holy Spirit down to you, but I can bring Him to you only at your own invitation. The Holy Spirit is in your right mind, as He was in mine. The Bible says, 'May the mind be in you that was also in Christ Jesus,' and uses this as a blessing. It is the blessing of miracle-mindedness. It asks that you may think as I thought, joining with me in Christ thinking." (T-5.I.3:2-6)

"As a man and also one of God's creations, my right thinking, which came from the Holy Spirit or the Universal Inspiration [Who I like to call God's Divine Psychiatrist], taught me first and foremost that this Inspiration is for all. I could not have It myself without knowing this." (T-5.I.4:6-7)

"It is possible even in this world to hear only that Voice [i.e., the Holy Spirit's Voice] and no other. It takes effort and great willingness to learn. It is the final lesson that I learned, and God's Sons are as equal as learners as they are as Sons." (T-5.II.3:9-11) Note that Jesus is telling all of us that if he was able to do it, so can we.

"My mind will always be like yours, because we were created as equals." (T-5.II.9:1)

"I am your model for decision. By deciding for God I showed you that this decision can be made, and that you can make it." (T-5.II.9:6-7)

"Believe with me, and we will become equal as teachers." (T-6.I.6:11)

We all started in God's Kingdom (Heaven). Then we made up another kingdom, we call the world, and which we all believed in although this world consists only of illusions. In the following paragraph, Jesus speaks of these two kingdoms: "Truth is without illusions and therefore within the Kingdom. Everything outside the Kingdom is illusion. When you threw truth away you saw yourself as if you were without it. By making another kingdom that you valued, you did not keep *only* the Kingdom of God in your mind, and thus placed part of your mind outside it. What you made has imprisoned your will, and given you a sick mind that must be healed. Your vigilance against this sickness is the way to heal it. Once your mind is healed it radiates health, and thereby teaches healing. This establishes you as a teacher who teaches like me. Vigilance was required of me as much as of you, and those who teach the same thing must be in agreement about what they believe." (T-6.V.C.9:1-9) In summary, simply believe only Heaven is real and never believe the world is real.

"When I said 'I am with you always,' I meant it literally." (T-7.III.1:7)

"If you want to be like me I will help you, knowing that we are alike. If you want to be different, I will wait until you change your mind. I can teach you, but only you can choose to listen to my teaching. How else can it be, if God's Kingdom is freedom? Freedom cannot be learned by tyranny of any kind, and the perfect equality of all God's Sons cannot be recognized through the dominion of one mind over another. God's Sons are equal in will, all being the Will of their Father. This is the only lesson I came to teach." (T-8.IV.6:3-9)

"By joining your mind with mine you are signifying your awareness that the Will of God is One." (T-8.V.2:12)

"You have surely begun to realize that this is a very practical course, and one that means exactly what it says. I would not ask you to do things you cannot do, and it is impossible that I could do things you cannot do. Given this, and given this quite literally, nothing can prevent you from doing exactly what I ask, and everything argues *for* your doing it. I give you no limits because God lays none upon you. When you limit yourself we are not of one mind, and that is sickness. Yet sickness is not of the body, but of the mind. All forms of sickness are signs that the mind is split, and does not accept a unified purpose." (T-8.IX.8:1-7)

"When you do not value yourself you become sick, but my value of you can heal you, because the value of God's Son is one. When I said, 'My peace I give unto you,' I meant it. Peace comes from God through me to you. It is for you although you may not ask for it." (T-10.III.6:5-8)

"My brother, you are part of God and part of me. When you have at last looked at the ego's foundation without shrinking you will also have looked upon ours. I come to you from our Father to offer you everything [i.e., Heaven] again. Do not refuse it in order to keep a dark cornerstone hidden, for its protection will not save you. I give you the lamp and I will go with you. You will not take this journey alone. I will lead you to your true Father, Who hath need of you, as I have. Will you not answer the call of love with joy?" (T-11.Intro.4:1-8)

"Teach not that I died in vain. Teach rather that I did not die by demonstrating that I live in you." (T-11.VI.7:3-4)

"God's Son *is* saved. Bring only this awareness to the Sonship, and you will have a part in the redemption as valuable as mine." (T-11.VI.10:1-2) After my first study of the *Course* many years ago, I understood that all of us here on earth would be "returning" to Heaven without exception. We are in fact all "saved" yet only a very small percentage of us are aware of this. The idea, taught by some religions, that some persons will end up spending their eternity in hell contradicts this *Course* idea 100%.

"Beautiful child of God, you are asking only for what I promised you. Do you believe I would deceive you? The Kingdom of Heaven *is* within you. Believe that the truth is in me, for I know that it is in you. God's Sons have nothing they do not share." (T-11.VIII.8:1-5)

"Blessed are you who teach with me. Our power comes not of us, but of our Father. In guiltlessness we know Him, as He knows us guiltless [for that is how He created us]. I stand within the circle, calling you to peace. Teach peace with me, and stand with me on holy ground. Remember for everyone your Father's power that He has given him [i.e., everyone in the world]. Believe not that you cannot teach His perfect peace. Stand not outside, but join with me within. Fail not the only purpose to which my teaching calls you. Restore to God His Son as He created him, by teaching him his innocence." (T-14.V.9:1-10)

"Be humble before Him [God], and yet great *in* Him. And value no plan of the ego before the plan of God. For you leave empty your place in His plan, which you must fill if you would join with me, by your decision to join in any plan but His. I call you to fulfill your holy part in the plan that He has given to the world for its release from littleness. God would have His host [the minds of all people and all life] abide in perfect freedom. Every allegiance to a plan of salvation apart from Him diminishes the value of His Will for you in your own mind. And yet it is your mind that is the host to Him." (T-15.IV.3:1-7)

"Turn with me firmly away from all illusions now, and let nothing stand in the way of truth. We will take the last useless journey away from truth together, and then together we go straight to God, in joyous answer to His Call for His completion." (T-16.IV.12:5-6)

"Return with me to Heaven, walking together with your brother out of this world and through another, to the loveliness and joy the other holds within it." (T-18.I.12:4) When we allow Jesus to be our teacher and friend, he is here to help us in all our relationships with other people helping us mend all bad relationships and making new relationships. As we literally join his mind, we find that we truly don't have an enemy in the world. Everyone in the world is either a friend or a potential friend waiting to be met. This has been my own experience.

"I hold your hand as surely as you agreed to take your brother's. You will not separate, for I stand with you and walk with you in your advance to truth. And where we go we carry God with us." (T-18.III.5:5-7)

The following paragraph, taken from one of the lessons, talks to me specifically and tells me that Jesus and I are a team which has an important mission: "We [Jesus and I] have a mission here. We did not come to reinforce the madness that we once believed in. [The world is truly an insane place.] Let us not forget the goal that we accepted. It is more than just our happiness alone we came to gain [though this is certainly a byproduct]. What we accept as what we are proclaims what everyone must be, along with us [We are all, collectively and individually, Christ, God's one Son or one Creation.] Fail not your brothers, or you fail yourself [because they are God's Son, too, the same as Jesus and me]. Look lovingly on them, that they may know that they are part of you, and you of them." (W-139.9:1-7)

Here's another Workbook quote where Jesus summarizes how he helps lead us out of this mad world of illusions: "I take the journey with you. For I share your doubts and fears a little while, that you may come to me who recognize the road by which all fears and doubts are overcome. We walk together. I must understand uncertainty and pain, although I know they have no meaning. Yet a savior must remain with those he teaches, seeing what they see, but still retaining in his mind the way that led him out, and now will lead you out with him. God's Son is crucified until you walk along the road with me." (W-Review V.Intro.6:1-6)

The last time I studied the 3-page Introduction to Part II of the Workbook for Students, about 2 months ago, I had a very interesting experience which should be instructive to other students of the *Course*.

By the way, this Introduction is located right after Lesson 220 of the Workbook. In these 3 pages, Jesus uses the words we, us, our, and ourselves a total of 86 times. In the world, these words generally mean physically together such as "We went to the movies." When I was reading these pages 2 months ago, I knew they meant "me and Jesus together" and I felt so close to Jesus that I was right there with him - in my mind, of course. This is the experience I'm sharing with you and, for me, it's the result of 18 years of diligent study of the *Course,* including 14 times doing the Workbook Lessons, one day at a time.

As Jesus tells us elsewhere in his *Course*: *"I am with you always"*. This is absolutely true but if we decide not to listen to him, he of course can't help us. However, he waits patiently until we do start listening to him. In the first sentence of paragraph 6 of the *Course*'s Introduction to Part II of the Workbook for Students, he says "I am so close to you we cannot fail." I fully believe Jesus here although, as I have indicated elsewhere in this book, I have not yet attained "complete forgiveness." However, I have clearly made wonderful progress in letting Jesus be my guide rather than the insane voice of the ego. Jesus is so close to me now, I'm convinced I can't fail.

Paragraph 2 of Lesson 221 reinforces this relationship I currently have with Jesus as do many of the subsequent lessons in Part II. "Now do we [Jesus and me] wait in quiet. God is here, because we wait together. I [Jesus] am sure that He will speak to you [Jimmy], and you will hear. Accept my confidence, for it is yours. Our minds are joined. [My mind is joined with Jesus' mind.] We wait with one intent; to hear our Father's answer to our call, to let our thoughts be still and find His peace, to hear Him speak to us of what we are, and to reveal Himself unto His Son." (W-221.2:1-6)

In the following paragraph, Jesus asks us to spend some time together just with him: "Let us come daily to this holy place, and spend a while together. Here we share our final dream. It is a dream in which there is no sorrow, for it holds a hint of all the glory given us by God. The grass is pushing through the soil, the trees are budding now, and birds have come to live within their branches. Earth is being born again in new perspective. Night has gone, and we have come together in the light." (W-Q 2.4:1-6)

In the following, Jesus is talking directly to me and I know he's telling me the truth. Further, I know it's true for everyone else in the world. "Brother, come and let me look on you. Your loveliness reflects my own. Your sinlessness is mine. You stand forgiven, and I stand with you." (W-247.1:5-8)

Here is Jesus' simple yet perfectly true definition for "the Word of God": "What is the Word of God? 'My Son is pure and holy as Myself.' And thus did God become the Father of the Son He loves, for thus was he created." (W-276.1:1-3) We are all an eternal part of God's Son and 100% innocent. What about this world? This world, which is all illusion, was made by the ego to block the knowledge of God and our own true Identity from us. All people born into this world initially believed this world was 100% real and the vast majority of people continue to believe it. With the Holy Spirit's help, the first individual to see through *all* of the ego's blocks was, of course, Jesus. In the end we will all wake up at Home in Heaven and this dream world will literally disappear.

If you haven't already noted this, be aware that in the Manual for Teachers Jesus is generally referenced in the third person. The way I think of this is that the Holy Spirit is the author of the Manual for Teachers. As the *Course* tells us, Jesus is the manifestation of the Holy Spirit. ["I am the manifestation of the Holy Spirit, and when you see me it will be because you have invited Him." (T-12.VII.6:1)] By the way, when we are thinking with our spirit mind, and not our ego mind, we too are the manifestation of the Holy Spirit. Also note that the Voice for God within our mind will be the same whether we think of the Voice as coming from Jesus, the Holy Spirit or Christ for the simple reason that they are all one.

"DOES JESUS HAVE A SPECIAL PLACE IN HEALING?" (M-23.title) The *Course* uses two pages to answer this question. As you study these 2 pages, you appreciate that the answer is: "Most emphatically yes!"

"Even the most advanced of God's teachers will give way to temptation in this world." (M-23.1:2) It is clear that this includes Jesus himself, the most advanced teacher of God 2,000 years ago. For instance, as Jesus was walking around with his disciples, some aspect of this world that he hadn't considered could cross his mind which seemed inviting to him and, getting ongoing input from the Holy Spirit, the Holy Spirit might have corrected him by saying: "Remember, the world you see holds *nothing* that you want (from Lesson 128). We're heading home to Heaven." This all would have likely happened within a few seconds and Jesus may never have shared it with anyone else; on the other hand, he may have shared it with his 12 friends.

What has been literally happening for me as I study Jesus' mind training course is that my mind is becoming one with Jesus' mind and it's been a most wonderful experience that can't be expressed in words. Since Jesus today is one with the Holy Spirit and with Christ, and They are one with our Father, my joining my mind with Jesus' mind is literally joining me with God and Heaven. The following quotes from Chapter 23 of the Manual for Teachers reinforce the importance of Jesus to me and other *Course* students:

> "We have repeatedly said that one [Jesus] who has perfectly accepted the Atonement for himself can heal the world. Indeed, he has already done so. Temptation may recur to others, but never to this One. He has become the risen Son of God. He has overcome death because he has accepted life. He has recognized himself as God created him, and in so doing he has recognized all living things as part of him. There is now no limit on his power, because it is the power of God. So has his name become the Name of God, for he no longer sees himself as separate from Him.

> "What does this mean for you? It means that in remembering Jesus you are remembering God. The whole relationship of the Son to the Father lies in him. His part in the Sonship is also yours, and his completed learning guarantees your own success. Is he still available for help? What did he say about this? [Answer – 'I am with you always.'] Remember his promises, and ask yourself honestly whether it is likely that he will fail to keep them. Can God fail His Son? And can one who is one with God be unlike Him? Who transcends the body has transcended limitation. Would the greatest teacher be unavailable to those who follow him?" (M-23.2:1 – 3:11)

"No one who has become a true and dedicated teacher of God forgets his brothers. Yet what he can offer them is limited by what he learns himself. Then turn to one [Jesus] who laid all limits by, and went beyond the farthest reach of learning. He will take you with him, for he did not go alone. And you were with him then, as you are now.

"This course has come from him [Jesus] because his words have reached you in a language you can love and understand. Are other teachers possible, to lead the way to those who speak in different tongues and appeal to different symbols? Certainly there are. Would God leave anyone without a very present help in time of trouble; a savior who can symbolize Himself? Yet do we need a many-faceted curriculum, not because of content differences, but because symbols must shift and change to suit the need. Jesus has come to answer yours. In him you find God's Answer. Do you, then, teach with him, for he is with you; he is always here." (M-23.6:6–7:8)

As I have indicated previously, I have not attained "complete forgiveness" status yet (which means to me I'm not yet in the "real world"). However, I have made significant "spiritual progress" which, in a nutshell, means that my peace of mind and happiness today is miraculously better than it was when I first started studying the *Course*. Further, my peace and happiness continue to improve with time. Based on my experience, I definitely encourage others interested in the *Course* to give it a good amount of time each day and continue doing so over an extended period of time. Here's the paradox: To get really happy, get really serious – in studying the *Course*. I tell you this as a preface to the following paragraph although it does not specifically mention the happiness evolution which occurs:

"Do not despair, then, because of limitations. It is your function to escape from them, but not to be without them. If you would be heard by those who suffer, you must speak their language. If you would be a savior, you must understand what needs to be escaped. Salvation is not theoretical. Behold the problem, ask for the answer [from Jesus I suggest], and then accept it when it comes. Nor will its coming be long delayed. All the help you can accept will be provided, and not one need you have will not be met. Let us not, then, be too concerned with goals for which you are not ready. God takes you where you are and welcomes you. What more could you desire, when this is all you need?" (M-26.4:1-11)

One of the best summaries of the *Course*, including the essential role Jesus plays, is contained in Chapter 5 of the Clarification of Terms. It is entitled "JESUS – CHRIST." Following are all 6 paragraphs of this chapter:

"1. There is no need for help to enter Heaven for you have never left [i.e., the world never happened]. But there is need for help beyond yourself as you are circumscribed by false beliefs of your Identity, which God alone established in reality [i.e., in Heaven]. Helpers are given you in many forms, although upon the altar they are one. Beyond each one there is a Thought of God, and this will never change. But they have names which differ for a time, for time needs symbols, being itself unreal. [Eternity is real. Time is not – it's just part of the illusion. Thus, like the world, time never happened.] Their names are legion, but we will not go beyond the names the course itself employs. God does not help because He knows no need. But He creates all Helpers of His Son while he believes his fantasies are true. [Most specifically, God created the Holy Spirit (also referred to as the Voice for God) to wake us from our dreams.] Thank God for them for they will lead you home [to Heaven].

"2. The name of *Jesus* is the name of one who was a man but saw the face of Christ in all his brothers and remembered God. So he became identified with *Christ*, a man no longer, but at one with God. The man was an illusion [as are all people], for he seemed to be a separate being, walking by himself, within a body that appeared to hold his self from Self [Christ, God's only Son], as all illusions do. Yet who can save unless he sees illusions and then identifies them as what they are? Jesus remains a Savior because he saw the false without accepting it as true. And Christ needed his form that He might appear to men and save them from their own illusions.

"3. In his complete identification with the Christ – the perfect Son of God, His one creation and His happiness, forever like Himself and one with Him – Jesus became what all of you must be. He led the way for you to follow him. He leads you back to God because he saw the road before him, and he followed it. He made a clear distinction, still obscure to you, between the false and true. He offered you a final demonstration that it is impossible to kill God's Son [when he physically returned two days after the world killed his body]; nor can his life in any way be changed by sin and evil, malice, fear or death [which is true for everyone else too].

"4. And therefore all your sins have been forgiven because they carried no effects at all. And so they were but dreams. [Since the entire world is a dream, naturally all our sins were dreams too and never happened.] Arise with him [Jesus] who showed you this because you owe him this who shared your dreams that they might be dispelled. And shares them still, to be at one with you. [Remember Jesus' promise: 'I am with you always.']

"5. Is he the Christ? O yes, along with you. His little life on earth was not enough to teach the mighty lesson that he learned for all of you. He will remain with you to lead you from the hell you made to God. And when you join your will with his, your sight will be his vision, for the eyes of Christ are shared. Walking with him is just as natural as walking with a [loving] brother whom you knew since you were born, for such indeed he is. Some bitter idols have been made of him who would be only brother to the [illusionary and insane] world. Forgive him your illusions, and behold how dear a brother he would be to you. For he will set your mind at rest at last and carry it with you unto your God.

"6. Is he God's only Helper? No, indeed. For Christ takes many forms with different names until their oneness can be recognized. But Jesus is for you the bearer of Christ's single message of the Love of God. You need no other. It is possible to read his words and benefit from them without accepting him into your life [i.e., into your mind]. Yet he would help you a little more if you will share your pains and joys with him, and leave them both to find the peace of God. Yet still it is his lesson most of all that he would have you learn, and it is this [from Jesus to us]:

> *"There is no death because the Son of God is like his Father. Nothing you can do can change Eternal Love. Forget your dreams of sin and guilt, and come with me [Jesus] instead to share the resurrection of God's Son. And bring with you all those whom He has sent to you to care for as I care for you."*
> (C-5.1:1–6:12)

In Chapter 6 of the Clarification of terms, entitled "The Holy Spirit", the importance of Jesus to the world's salvation is clearly made: "He [the Holy Spirit] has established Jesus as the leader in carrying out His plan since he was the first to complete his own part perfectly." (C-6.2:2)

Chapter 3: Forgiveness

This chapter consists of 4 sections as follows:

Section A: Introduction

Forgiveness, as defined in the *Course*, means something totally different than what the word means before one studies the *Course*. Unless otherwise stated, in this book the words forgive, forgiveness, forgiven, forgiving, etc. are based on Jesus' definition from his *Course*. To the best of my knowledge, Jesus' definition is different than any other and can only be found in his *Course*.

Section B: My personal experience in forgiving

Following my first time through the *Course many years ago,* I intellectually had a good idea of what forgiveness meant which was that this world I've been living in is but a dream that I made up; it's not real at all. Given this, I shouldn't get angry or annoyed or take the world seriously. I will eventually wake up and be back home in eternal Heaven, living happily ever after and so will everyone else in the world. In a nutshell, the world is just an illusion – it was never real, it's not real now and it won't be real in the future. Given this, forgiveness means "there's nothing to forgive."

While this all made sense to me, I still got angry, blamed others and took the world too seriously. However, I had made some progress even after the first go round of studying the Text and Manual for Teachers and doing the Workbook for Students. I was reacting less to the world and had more peace of mind. In other words, I had made some spiritual progress.

Now, many years later, after studying the Text and Manual for Teachers many times over and doing the Workbook for Students 13 more times, my spiritual progress has been wonderful. The result for me has been an ever increasing level of happiness and joy within my wonderful worldly life. Based on this experience, I encourage others to make the study of the *Course* "a way of life" as I have done.

Please note that in recent years, I also study the two short supplements (about 25 pages each) which were also authored by Jesus (*Psychotherapy: Purpose, Process and Practice* and *The Song of Prayer*). I study these after I finish studying the Manual for Teachers and I've found both to be very helpful.

As I indicated above, after my first study of the *Course* I understood intellectually what forgiveness meant and benefited somewhat in my daily life from that first study. Today, I am experiencing it in virtually all my daily affairs although I still sometimes get caught off guard by my ego thoughts. I think of myself as an advancing student/teacher of the *Course.*

Section C: The importance of forgiving

Lessons 62 through 66 of the Workbook for Students help us learn the importance of forgiveness. Their titles are as follows:

62. "Forgiveness is my function as the light of the world."

63. "The light of the world brings peace to every mind through my forgiveness."

64. "Let me not forget my function."

65. "My only function is the one God gave me."

66. "My happiness and my function are one."

These lessons tell me that, while I'm in this world, my only function is forgiveness which I should try not to forget because my happiness depends on it.

In the Manual for Teachers Jesus tells us that "Awareness of dreaming is the real function of God's teachers." (M-12.6:6) This might appear to contradict the preceding 5 lessons which tell me that "forgiveness" is my only function. However, forgiveness tells me that this entire world that I once thought was real is simply a dream that I made up in my mind and has "nothing" to do with reality. Given this, forgiveness allows me to clearly see that "there is nothing to forgive," which I mentioned above. It should also be clear that the terms "forgiveness" and "awareness of dreaming" mean the same thing.

I'll now finish paragraph 6 of Chapter 12 of the Manual for Teachers, beginning again with sentence 6: "Awareness of dreaming is the real function of God's teachers. They watch the dream figures come and go, shift and change, suffer and die. Yet they are not deceived by what they see. They recognize that to behold a dream figure as sick and separate is no more real than to regard it as healthy and beautiful. Unity alone |truth or Heaven| is not a thing of dreams. And it is this God's teachers acknowledge as behind the dream, beyond all seeming and yet surely theirs." (M-12.6:6-11)

In the wording of the *Course*, Jesus often uses different words to express the same idea and tells us this in different parts of the *Course*. Recently, the *Course* has been greatly simplified for me by realizing that the following words mean the same thing: forgiveness, salvation, Atonement, true perception and healing. With regard to the first 4 terms from this list, Jesus tells us: "For true perception is a remedy with many names. Forgiveness, salvation, Atonement, true perception, all are one." (C-4.3:5-6) With regard to healing, Jesus tells us: "To forgive is to heal." (M-22.1:9) and two paragraphs later he tells us "That forgiveness is healing needs to be understood, if the teacher of God is to make progress." (M-22.3:1) Because this simplification has helped me so much, I've included the following chart:

When I see or think of Atonement, I think of - - - - - - - - forgiveness.

When I see or think of salvation, I think of - - - - - - - - - -forgiveness.

When I see or think of true perception, I think of - - - - - forgiveness.

When I see or think of healing, I think of - - - - - - - - - - - forgiveness.

Section D: Specific references to forgiveness

Following are some additional quotes from the *Course* on forgiveness:

"As we learn to recognize our perceptual errors, we also learn to look past them or 'forgive.'" (P-p.xi.2nd par: next to the last sentence)

"You who want peace can find it only by complete forgiveness." (T-1.VI.1:1)

"Once forgiveness has been accepted [completely], prayer in the usual sense becomes utterly meaningless. The prayer for forgiveness is nothing more than a request that you may be able to recognize what you already have [i.e., my only reality which is Heaven]." (T-3.V.6:4-5)

"Forgiveness is the healing of the perception of separation." (T-3.V.9:1)

"To forgive is to overlook." (T-9.IV.1:2)

"Forgiveness that is learned of me [Jesus] does not use fear to undo fear. Nor does it make real the unreal [i.e., the world] and then destroy it." (T-9.IV.5:1-2)

"There is nothing to forgive." (T-14.III.7:5) There's nothing for me to forgive because this entire world is simply a dream made up by me with the ego part of my mind and has nothing to do with my reality.

"Ask, rather, to learn how to forgive, and to restore what always was to your unforgiving mind." (T-14.IV.3:5)

"And that in complete forgiveness, in which you recognize that there is nothing to forgive, you are absolved completely." (T-15.VIII.1:7)

"Can you imagine how beautiful those you forgive will look to you? In no fantasy have you ever seen anything so lovely." (T-17.II.1:1-2)

"To forgive is merely to remember only the loving thoughts you gave in the past, and those that were given you. All the rest must be forgotten. Forgiveness is a selective remembering, based not on your selection." (T-17.III.1:1-3)

"Be willing to forgive the Son of God for what he did not do." (T-17.III.1:5) I really like passages like this because it tells me that this whole life of mine here on earth has been nothing but a dream coming from my mind so a couple of small grievances I still hold onto never happened. (I've also just told you that I haven't gotten to the "complete forgiveness" level yet.)

"Forgiveness removes only the untrue, lifting the shadows from the world and carrying it, safe and sure within its gentleness, to the bright world of new and clean perception. There is your purpose *now*. And it is there that peace awaits you." (T-18.IX.14:3-5)

"In kind forgiveness will the world sparkle and shine, and everything you once thought sinful now will be reinterpreted as part of Heaven." (T-23.Intro.6:4)

"Open the door of His most holy home, and let forgiveness sweep away all trace of the belief in sin that keeps God homeless and His Son with Him." (T-23.I.10:3) The power of forgiveness becomes clear in this sentence. Forgiveness means this world never happened. It's not real. There is no world! We are all 100% eternal innocent parts of God's Creation and all parts are in union with each other and in union with our Father. We are incredibly happy, joyous and free forever and ever. In conclusion, sin never happened. Although all of us believed in sin and death and pain and suffering at one point in time, we learn that it's all been a massive fictional play orchestrated by our sick ego minds. I say "Thank God this world isn't real!"

"Where could your peace arise *but* from forgiveness?" (T-24.V.3:1)

"Forgive your brother, and you cannot separate yourself from him nor from his Father. You need no forgiveness, for the wholly pure [God's Sons] have never sinned. Give, then, what He has given you, that you may see His Son as one, and thank his Father as He thanks you." (T-25.II.10:1-3)

"Forgiveness is the only function meaningful in time." (T-25.VI.5:3)

"That is why your sole responsibility must be to take forgiveness for yourself." (T-25.IX.9:6)

"Forgiveness thus becomes the means by which he [i.e., anyone] learns he has nothing to forgive." (T-26.IV.1:6)

"Forgiveness turns the world of sin into a world of glory, wonderful to see. Each flower shines in light, and every bird sings of the joy of Heaven. There is no sadness and there is no parting here, for everything is totally forgiven. And what has been forgiven must join, for nothing stands between to keep them separate and apart. The sinless must perceive that they are one, for nothing stands between to push the other off. And in the space that sin left vacant do they join as one, in gladness recognizing what is part of them has not been kept apart and separate." (T-26.IV.2:1-6) You must admit that this paragraph offers a set of promises that most individuals would call insane. For students of the *Course*, it tells us why we want to continue to train our minds as it prescribes because by so doing our happiness continues to increase. Leastwise, this has been my own experience. I admit that currently I do not have complete forgiveness but I have made a lot of progress towards that end so that I am becoming ever happier over time.

"Forgiveness is the great release from time. It is the key to learning that the past is over." (T-26.V.6:1-2) The past is over because it was just a dream and never really happened.

"Forgive the past and let it go, for it *is* gone." (T-26.V.14:1)

"Forgiveness is the only function here, and serves to bring the joy this world denies to every aspect of God's Son where sin was thought to rule." (T-26.VII.8:5)

"What is forgiveness but a willingness that truth be true." (T-26.VII.10:3)

"Forgiveness is the answer to attack of any kind." (T-26.VII.17:2)

"Who forgives is healed." (T-27.II.3:10)

"Correction must be left to One [Jesus/Holy Spirit/Christ] Who knows correction and forgiveness are the same." (T-27.II.16:1) Here we see that another *Course* word that means the same as forgiveness is "correction."

"Forgiveness separates the dreamer [you and me] from the evil dream, and thus releases him." (T-28.V.3:3)

"So perfectly can you forgive him [anyone, especially someone I have a grievance against] his illusions he becomes your savior from your dreams." (T-29.III.3:5)   This reinforces my thinking that those individuals who appear to give me the most trouble are my best teachers (or saviors).

"Whom you forgive is given power to forgive you your illusions. By your gift of freedom is it given unto you." (T-29.III.3:12-13)

"On earth this [the extension of love] means forgive your brother, that the darkness may be lifted from your mind." (T-29.III.4:2)

"Forgiveness is your peace, for herein lies the end of separation and the dream of danger and destruction, sin and death; of madness and of murder, grief and loss." (T-29.VI.1:4)

"Forgiveness, once complete, brings timelessness so close the song of Heaven can be heard, not with the ears, but with the holiness that never left the altar that abides forever deep within the Son of God." (T-29.IX.8:5) For me, the term "altar" is more simply understood to mean "the remembrance of Heaven or of God" which each of us maintains within our minds.

"Salvation [i.e., forgiveness] is a paradox indeed! What could it be except a happy dream? It asks you but that you forgive all things that no one ever did; to overlook what is not there, and not to look upon the unreal as reality. You are but asked to let your will [which is the same as God's] be done, and seek no longer for the things you do not want. And you are asked to let yourself be free of all the dreams of what you never were, and seek no more to substitute the strength of idle wishes for the Will of God." (T-30.IV.7:1-5)

"The real world is the state of mind in which the only purpose of the world is seen to be forgiveness." (T-30.V.1:1)

"And all that stood between your image of yourself and what you are [in truth], forgiveness washes joyfully away." (T-30.V.6:2)

"Forgive your brother all appearances, that are but ancient lessons you have taught yourself about the sinfulness in you." (T-31.II.9:1)   Of course, the lessons you taught yourself about your own sinfulness came from the ego part of your mind because in truth we are all 100% innocent.

"The key to forgiveness lies in it [i.e., the idea that 'my meaningless thoughts are showing me a meaningless world']." (W-11.1:5)

"*I see through the eyes of forgiveness.*" (W-43.5:4) The title of this 43rd lesson is: "God is my Source. I cannot see apart from Him." When we "see through the eyes of forgiveness" we see right through this dream world, fully understanding it's not real, and find ourselves at the gate of Heaven. Our Source, God, is of course right there at the gate with us.

"God is the Love in which I forgive." (W-46.title) "Forgiveness is the great need of this world, but that is because it is a world of illusions. Those who forgive are thus releasing themselves from illusions, while those who withhold forgiveness are binding themselves to them. As you condemn only yourself, so do you forgive only yourself." (W-46.1:3-5)

"For this reason [i.e., forgiveness undoes all fear thus returning our minds to God], forgiveness can truly be called salvation. It is the means by which illusions disappear." (W-46.2:4-5)

"As forgiveness allows love to return to my awareness, I will see a world of peace and safety and joy. And it is this I choose to see, in place of what I look on now." (W-55.3:4-5) Here's a real good reason to continue learning forgiveness from Jesus and his *Course*.

"Yet forgiveness is the means by which I will recognize my innocence." (W-60.1:4) Forgiveness is also the way we recognize that everyone else is innocent too. This leads us back to the great paradoxical definition of forgiveness which is "there is nothing to forgive."

"There is not a moment in which God's Voice [Jesus/Holy Spirit/Christ] ceases to call on my forgiveness to save me." (W-60.4:2) It is important to recognize that God loves us all equally and unbelievably. He has no favorites. This is why Jesus says early in the Text: "'Many are called but few are chosen' should be, 'All are called but few choose to listen.' Therefore, they do not choose right. The 'chosen ones' are merely those who choose right sooner [Jesus was the first to do so and, at the end of time, all of us will have done so]. Right minds can do this now and they will find rest unto their souls. God knows you only in peace, and this *is* your reality." (T-3.IV.7:12-16)

"I am the light of the world. That is my only function. That is why I am here." (W-61.5:3-5) Quite explicitly, Jesus is telling us that our only function here on earth is to "be the light of the world" just as he was two thousand years ago. In many other places in his *Course* he tells us forgiveness is our only function. As we experience the *Course's* teachings on an increasing basis, we appreciate that there is no contradiction here. Once we achieve complete forgiveness, we only listen to God's Voice (Jesus/Holy Spirit/Christ) and completely ignore the ego's voice (though we might slip once in a while). When we only listen to God's Voice, we have the same mind as Jesus did (and still does) and we become the "light of the world" also. So another definition for forgiveness (or complete forgiveness) is "to be the light of the world."

"Forgiveness is my function as the light of the world. I would fulfill my function that I may be happy." (W-62.5:2-3) My experience over the many years I've been studying the *Course* is that my level of happiness has increased unbelievably and continues to increase. However, I know I have not attained complete forgiveness because I still get annoyed and impatient at times. It's perfectly clear to me, however, that I've been listening to God's Voice on an increasing basis and listening to the world's voice (i.e., the ego's voice) on a decreasing basis. My increasing happiness is directly related to this changing mind of mine which, in turn, is directly related to my ongoing studies in the *Course*. My hope is that I'll stop holding onto some things I think this world can offer me and thereby attain complete forgiveness (i.e., fulfill my function 100%). Following is a modified version of the quote at the beginning of this paragraph which tells you and me where I'm at today: "Complete forgiveness is my function as the light of the world. I hope that I will completely fulfill my function soon that I will be happy every second of every day and night."

"Let me not forget my function [This is the title of Lesson 64]. *Let me not try to substitute mine for God's. Let me forgive and be happy."* (W-64.6:2-4) What these few sentences tell us is that another word the *Course* uses

to define "forgiveness" is "happiness". Jesus tells us this explicitly in the simple title of Lesson 66: "My happiness and my function are one."

Lesson 78 helps us to see those persons we have grievances (i.e., resentments) against through the eyes of forgiveness. The title of this Lesson is "Let miracles replace all grievances." (W-78.title) Paragraph 7 of this lesson reads as follows:

> "7. Then let us ask of Him [the Holy Spirit] Who knows this Son of God in his reality and truth, that we may look on him a different way, and see our savior [i.e., the person we have a grievance against] shining in the light of true forgiveness [i.e., complete forgiveness], given unto us. We ask Him in the holy Name of God and of His Son, as holy as Himself:
>
> > *Let me behold my savior in this one You have appointed as the one for me to ask to lead me to the holy light in which he stands, that I may join with him.*
>
> The body's eyes are closed, and as you think of him who grieved you, let your mind be shown the light in him beyond your grievances." (W-78.7:1-4) My own experience in the *Course* is that those persons I have had my worst grievances or resentments against (i.e., those who I've felt have done me the most harm) have been, without a doubt, my best teachers. It's perfectly clear to me also that once I've attained "complete forgiveness" I can't possibly have any grievances against anyone or anything.

"*This* [e.g., something that disturbs me] *cannot separate my happiness from my function* [forgiveness]. *The oneness of my happiness and my function remains wholly unaffected by this. Nothing, including this, can justify the illusion of happiness apart from my function.*" (W-83.4:2-4) To understand this better, we must remember that the world we think we live in is but a dream and is not at all real. As Jesus tells us "There is no world! This is the central thought the course attempts to teach." (W-132.6:2-3) Of course this also means there never was a world and there will never be a world. In fact, we have all been "dreaming an impossible dream." So my happiness should not at all be interrupted by anything external to me – my happiness is 100% an inside job. With all this in mind, note the following examples:

If something bad happens in your worldly life, it didn't.

If something tragic happens in your worldly life, it didn't.

If something good happens in your worldly life, it didn't.

If something wonderful happens in your worldly life, it didn't.

"My function here is to forgive the world for all the errors I have made. For thus am I released from them with all the world." (W-115.1:2-3) Our ego minds are extremely powerful. For instance, my ego mind made up every aspect of this world – it made up my body, my parents, my friends and enemies over the years and my 3 marriages and 4 children. Further, it made up a history of my world, including Jesus, Hitler, Mother Theresa, Ken Wapnick and Donald Trump. It made up the idea of time and the physical universe which seemed to tell me that there is an infinite physical universe reaching out beyond our solar system and the furthest stars we can "see" with our most powerful telescopes. All these are simply errors I have made and, with the help of Jesus/Holy Spirit/Christ I must, and I will, undo them all. One of the simplest definitions of forgiveness is that this entire life I think I've been living is but a dream I made up and once I completely wake up (i.e., have complete forgiveness) I'll be seeing the gate of Heaven all the time. I won't be seeing Heaven's gate with my physical eyes, of course, because these eyes are part of my dream and aren't real. I'll be seeing beyond my dream world using Christ's vision. So as I make spiritual progress, any new enemies I think I have are easily dispelled by simply recognizing I made them up. It's all one massive egotistical life coming solely from the insane part of my mind. Once I've "mastered" the *Course* teachings, I will have completely forgiven my entire dream world and, of course, everyone who appears to be in it.

"Forgiveness is the key to happiness." (W-121.title)

"Forgiveness offers everything I want." (W-122.title)

"Forgiveness is the only thing that stands for truth in the illusions of the world." (W-134.7:1)

"By its [refers to forgiveness] ability to overlook what is not there, it opens up the way to truth [or Heaven's gate], which has been blocked by dreams of guilt." (W-134.8:3) In general, guilt refers to being angry at oneself and blame refers to being angry at someone or something else. In his *Course*, where Jesus uses the word "guilt", he wants us to be thinking "blame" also. The mistake is the same – it's referred to as attack or anger and it matters not whether you're angry at yourself or someone or something you believe is outside yourself. To wake up from your dream, you must be rid of anger entirely.

"I feel the Love of God within me now." (W-189.title) For the vast majority of people in the world today, the world is real. I too, of course, thought the same way for most of my life. I can't imagine that people who believe the world is real can have any understanding of the "Love of God." Now that I know that this world is in fact a dream and has nothing to do with God's Love and I am waking up from my dream, this lesson is perfectly clear to me. The first 3 paragraphs of this lesson tell of these two different views of the world:

> "There is a light in you the world can not perceive. And with its eyes you will not see this light, for you are blinded by the world. Yet you have eyes to see it. It is there for you to look upon. It was not placed in you to be kept hidden from your sight. This light is a reflection of the thought we practice now. To feel the Love of God within you is to see the world anew, shining in innocence, alive with hope, and blessed with perfect charity and love.

> "Who could feel fear in such a world as this? It welcomes you, rejoices that you came, and sings your praises as it keeps you safe from every form of danger and of pain. It offers you a warm and gentle home in which to stay a while. It blesses you throughout the day, and watches through the night as silent guardian of your holy sleep. It sees salvation in you, and protects the light in you, in which it sees its own. It offers you its flowers and its snow, in thankfulness for your benevolence.

> "This is the world the Love of God reveals. It is so different from the world you see through darkened eyes of malice and of fear, that one belies the other. Only one can be perceived at all. The other one is wholly meaningless. A world in which forgiveness shines on everything, and peace offers its gentle light to everyone, is inconceivable to those who see a world of hatred rising from attack, poised to avenge, to murder and destroy." (W-189.1:1–3:5)

"Forgiveness represents your function here. It is not God's creation, for it is the means by which untruth can be undone. And who would pardon Heaven? Yet on earth, you need to let illusions [i.e., dreams] go. Creation merely waits for your return to be acknowledged, not to be complete." (W-192.2:3-7) What this last sentence tells us is that Creation, or Christ, has never lost His completion even though we fell asleep. He's merely waiting for us to wake up from our dreams (i.e., to learn and practice complete forgiveness). This Lesson 192, by the way, includes two pages of wonderful information on the positive power of forgiveness.

"When your forgiveness is complete you will have total gratitude, for you will see that everything has earned the right to love by being loving, even as your Self." (W-195.8:6) In the *Course,* the word "Self" refers to God's one Son (which has the same meaning as Christ or God's one Creation). Please note that when the *Course* uses the term "self" (lower case) it is referring to our illusionary individual identities here in the world. Thus for me, my self is Jimmy Laws, which has nothing to do with who I am in truth, and my Self (or your Self) is Christ, God's one Son and one Creation, Who I am (and you are) in truth.

"Forgiveness is the end of dreams, because it is a dream of waking. It is not itself the truth. Yet does it point to where the truth must be, and gives direction with the certainty of God Himself. It is a dream in which the Son of God awakens to his Self and to his Father, knowing They are one." (W-198.3:4-7)

The following paragraph truly answers the question "Why should I learn forgiveness?"

> "What does forgiveness do? In truth [i.e., in Heaven] it has no function, and does nothing. For it is unknown in Heaven. It is only hell [i.e., earth] where it is needed, and where it must serve a mighty function. Is not the escape of God's beloved Son from evil dreams that he imagines, yet believes are true, a worthy purpose? Who could hope for more, while there appears to be a choice to make between success and failure; love and fear?" (W-200.6:1-6)

The following paragraph tells us what the world is and explains how forgiveness is the solution to all its apparent problems:

"The world is false perception. It is born of error, and it has not left its source [i.e., the ego]. It will remain no longer than the thought that gave it birth is cherished. When the thought of separation has been changed to one of true [or complete] forgiveness, will the world be seen in quite another light; and one which leads to truth, where all the world must disappear and all its errors vanish. Now its source [the ego and its idea of separation from God] has gone, and its effects are gone as well." (W-Q 3.1:1-5)

"Without forgiveness I will still be blind." (W-247.title) Clearly, Jesus is not referring to physical blindness here. In today's world, the vast majority of people are "blind" because they lack spiritual sight. (Everyone will eventually acquire it and fully wake up at Home in Heaven.) The term Jesus uses in his *Course* for spiritual sight is "Christ's vision" (and often just "vision"). This is discussed further in the next quote.

"For forgiveness is the only means whereby Christ's vision comes to me." (W-247.1:3) Christ's vision, of course, has nothing to do with the body's eyes which are just a part of our dream world. Following are two ways I use Christ's vision – (1) To see through this entire physical world to the gate of Heaven and (2) To see all human beings, including myself, as God's one Son (or Christ). What this quote tells us is that as our "forgiveness" increases so does our Christ vision increase.

"The way to God is through forgiveness here. There is no other way." (W-256.1:1-2) This quote succinctly and definitively tells us how important forgiveness is.

"Today I choose to see a world forgiven, in which everyone shows me the face of Christ, and teaches me that what I look upon belongs to me; that nothing is, except Your holy Son." (W-269.1:5) Heaven is a spiritual place; there are no bodies and there are no forms. God has no face; His Son, Christ, has no face; and the Holy Spirit has no face. The *Course* tells me that you are Christ, I am Christ, and everyone in the world is Christ for the simple reason that "God has only one Son." This makes us all absolutely equal (as well as one) rather than the 7.5 billion struggling individuals the ego's world has most of us believing. The term "face of Christ", however, is even more expansive than this

important idea of the equality and oneness of all people. The "face of Christ" means that everything I perceive in this world, not just other people, are but dreams of mine and have no real meaning. As I give all these dreams to Christ, they fade before His glory which is also my own. Once I have accomplished this (i.e., once I have complete forgiveness), every aspect of this world becomes the "face of Christ" because all my dreams, though still perceived, are seen as nothing because my mind sees only God's one Son or one Creation. Following are 2 quotes from the Manual for Teachers which help define the all-inclusive nature of the term "face of Christ" as well as the importance of forgiveness:

> "How do the open-minded forgive? They have let go all things that would prevent forgiveness. They have in truth abandoned the world, and let it be restored to them in newness and in joy so glorious they could never have conceived of such a change. Nothing is as it was formerly. Nothing but sparkles now which seemed so dull and lifeless before. And above all are all things welcoming, for threat has gone. No clouds remain to hide the face of Christ. Now is the goal achieved. Forgiveness is the final goal of the curriculum. It paves the way for what goes far beyond all learning. The curriculum makes no effort to exceed its legitimate goal. Forgiveness is its single aim, at which all learning ultimately converges. It is indeed enough." (M-4.X.2:1-13)

> "We have seen the face of Christ, His sinlessness, His Love behind all forms, beyond all purposes." (M-28.5:5)

"Father, my holiness is Yours. Let me rejoice in it, and through forgiveness be restored to sanity." (W-285.2:1-2) In his *Course*, Jesus describes two thought systems. The first is the one we're all born into which is the world's thought system with the ego as our guide. The other is the one we will all ultimately learn which is God's thought system with His Voice (Jesus/Holy Spirit/Christ) as our guide. The first is perfectly insane at every level and the second is perfectly sane at every level. In the quote above, the term *"be restored to sanity"* ultimately means to only follow the Voice for God.

"Father, forgiveness is the light You chose to shine away all conflict and all doubt, and light the way for our return to You. No light but this can end our evil dream. No light but this can save the world. For this alone

will never fail in anything, being Your gift to Your beloved Son." (W-333.2:1-4)

"Therefore forgiveness is the necessary condition for finding the peace of God. More than this, given forgiveness there *must* be peace." (M-20.3:6-7)

"Forgive the world, and you will understand that everything God created cannot have an end, and nothing He did not create is real. In this one sentence is our course [*A Course in Miracles*] explained." (M-20.5:7-8)

"Forgiveness, then, is all that need be taught, because it is all that need be learned. All blocks to the remembrance of God are forms of unforgiveness and nothing else." (Psy-2.II.3:2-3)

"Behold the greatest help [i.e., forgiveness] that God ordained to be with you until you reach to Him. Illusion's end will come with this. Unlike the timeless nature of its sister, prayer, forgiveness has an end. For it becomes unneeded when the rising up is done [and we're fully awake again in Heaven]. Yet now it has a purpose beyond which you cannot go, nor have you need to go. Accomplish this and you have been redeemed. Accomplish this and you will save the world." (Song-2.Intro.1:5-11)

"You have understood that you forgive and pray but for yourself [for the simple reason that God has only one Son]." (Song-3.IV.4:3)

Chapter 4: We are all one with our Father

This chapter consists of 2 sections as follows:

Section A: Overview ….. Begins on this page.

Section B: Specific references to oneness ….. page 41.

Section A: Overview

Approximately 2,000 years ago, Jesus said "I and the Father are one." What he clearly tells us now in his *Course* is that we are all one with the Father although very few believe this for the simple reason that we believe the world is real and not a dream that we made up. What Jesus tells us literally is that we made the world (it's our dream) and the world did not make us.

Another thing Jesus said two centuries ago was "The spirit gives life; the flesh counts for nothing." This is actually a wonderful summary of the *Course*. When God created us in Heaven as His Son, He gave us an eternal Spirit and it is something we all continue to have. Although it has been temporarily forgotten, eventually we will all remember it. So we can expand the first part of the Jesus Biblical quote to "The eternal spirit gives eternal life." What Jesus tells us in his *Course* is not only does the flesh (which I interpret as our bodies) count for nothing but the entire world counts for nothing. Jesus says this very succinctly in Lesson 132: "There is no world! This is the central thought the course attempts to teach." (W-132.6:2-3)

In his *Course*, Jesus tells us many times what truth is and, even better, provides us with a road map of how to get there. Truth is another name for Heaven where we will be happy, joyous and free forever and ever. We will all live happily ever after …. into eternal life.

For a while, Heaven consisted only of God. This was truth. Then God created His Creation (generally referred to as "His Son" in the *Course*) and They shared the same perfect and joyous Mind, which of course was eternal. So now Heaven consisted of two parts, God the Father and His Son, sharing the same eternal joyous Mind. The only difference was that the Father created the Son and the Son did not create the Father but, because They shared the same incredible joyous eternal Mind, this difference was of no consequence whatsoever in Heaven. In any event, truth (or Heaven) now consisted of two components joined as one – the Father and His Son. Clearly, We and the Father were one back then.

After a while, the Son had a tiny, mad idea which went something like "Let Me go off on my own without My Father." (This is referred to as the "separation" or "the idea of separation" in the *Course*.) Because God created perfect union between Himself and His Son for all eternity, it was literally impossible for His Son to separate. However, it was possible for His Son to "believe" He could separate. This belief caused the Son to fall into a deep sleep or coma in Heaven which Our Father, of course, immediately noticed.

Without any hesitation, our Father created the Holy Spirit, Whom I like to refer to as the Great Divine Psychiatrist, to go into His Son's dream and wake Him up. Right there and then the problem was solved although, for those of us who believe we're living on planet earth today, this is impossible to comprehend.

So now Heaven consists of three parts – Our Father and His two Creations, His Son and the Holy Spirit - which the *Course* refers to as the Holy Trinity. All three of Us share the same incredible joyous eternal Mind. To repeat this important simple fact, truth (or Heaven) now consists of three components joined as one – the Father, His Son, and the Holy Spirit.

Now, for those of us who believe we're on planet earth, where do we stand? In truth, each of us is part of God's one Son but we're caught up in a dream world (or a nightmare world) where everyone and everything is separate from each other and where eternal life has no applicability whatsoever. Everything in this world is the exact opposite of truth (Heaven). Thank God it's only a dream!

In his *Course*, Jesus sometimes uses the analogy of dreams we have when we're asleep at night. Suppose I'm asleep in my bed and I dream that I'm visiting Australia, which is a country I would really like to visit. (I think this love of Australia really took hold for me when I saw the first "Crocodile Dundee" movie.) When I wake up from my sleep and find I've never left my bed, I realize that I never went to Australia although it seemed 100% real while I was dreaming. In the same way, Jesus tells us, all 7.5 billion of us will eventually wake up from our worldly dreams and find ourselves back Home in Heaven which we never really left. We will all be one with each other, one with the Holy Spirit and one with our Father. The one Mind of God and His Creations is the only Reality.

We should, of course, thank God for the Holy Spirit Whose job is not completed until the last of us wakes up from his dreaming. Again, in his *Course*, Jesus tells us that there is a 100% guarantee that everyone will, in fact, wake up although it will likely take millions of years before the last of us accomplishes this.

Jesus is a very important individual because he was the first person to wake up from his dream before he physically left planet earth. As author of the *Course*, he tells us innumerable times throughout the *Course* that he's available to us all the time. He also tells us that, ultimately, he's just part of God's Son, the same as you and me. He makes the point that if he was able to listen only to the Holy Spirit when he was a man in the dream, and stop listening to the ego, then so can we but it takes a lot of training to do this. Personally, as a long term student of the *Course*, I know this to be true because I have been moving in this direction quite nicely.

Section B: Specific references to oneness

The truth that God's Mind and His Son's Mind are joined as one Mind is stated many times in the *Course*. The *Course* also notes many times that all people share the one Mind of God's one Son. In other words, all people are, in truth, Christ, God's only Child. Following are some of these references:

"In the realm of knowledge [Heaven] no thoughts exist apart from God, because God and His Creation share one Will." (P-p.x, "What It Says", 3rd par., 2nd sent.)

"It should especially be noted that God has only *one* Son. If all His creations are His Sons, every one must be an integral part of the whole Sonship." (T-2.VII.6:1-2)

"When the Will of the Sonship and the Father are one, their perfect accord is Heaven." (T-3.II.4:6)

"The Son of God is part of the Holy Trinity, but the Trinity Itself is One. There is no confusion within Its Levels, because They are of one Mind and one Will. This single purpose creates perfect integration and establishes the peace of God." (T-3.II.5:4-6)

"Knowledge [another term for Heaven] preceded both perception and time, and will ultimately replace them." (T-3.III.6:4)

"Only the oneness of knowledge is free of conflict." (T-3.VII.6:8) Elsewhere in the *Course*, Jesus tells us that "Conflict is the root of all evil." Although the Biblical Paul said the love of money was the root of all evil, he has been corrected by Jesus. Of course, money issues do cause a lot of conflict in this world so Paul wasn't too far off the mark.

"The Kingdom of Heaven *is* you." (T-4.III.1:4) Jesus starts out this paragraph with his Biblical quote "The Kingdom of Heaven is within you." Then he points out that the word "within" is both confusing and unnecessary. In Heaven, there is but one Mind, which we all have and are – Father, Son and Holy Spirit are one. You are Heaven, I am Heaven, everyone else is Heaven, our Father is Heaven and the Holy Spirit is Heaven. As the *Course* tells us, we are effectively God, the only difference is that God created us and we didn't create Him.

"Your mind is one with God's." (T-4.IV.2:7)

"The joint will of the Sonship [which is the one will of God's Son] is the only creator that can create like the Father, because only the complete can think completely, and the thinking of God lacks nothing." (T-5.IV.7:4)

"Each of us is the light of the world, and by joining our minds in this light we proclaim the Kingdom of God together and as one." (T-6.II.13:5) When my mind is joined with Jesus, which it is ever more frequently as a direct result of my studying his *Course*, "I am the light of the world." (Please note that this quote is the title of Lesson 61 of the Workbook.)

"You *are* the Will of God." (T-7.VII.10:1)

"Your will is as powerful as His [God's] because it *is* His." (T-7.X.4:8)

"When you have learned that your will is God's you could no more will to be without Him than He could will to be without you. This is freedom and this is joy." (T-8.II.6:4-5)

"Your identification is with the Father *and* with the Son. It cannot be with One and not the Other. If you are part of One you must be part of the Other, because They are One. The Holy Trinity is holy *because* It is One. If you exclude yourself from this union, you are perceiving the Holy Trinity as separated. You must be included in It, because It is everything." (T-8.IV.8:6-11)

"The undivided will of the Sonship [God's one Son or God's Creation] is the perfect creator, being wholly in the likeness of God, Whose Will it is." (T-8.V.2:1)

"By joining your mind with mine [Jesus] you are signifying your awareness that the Will of God is One." (T-8.V.2:12)

"Whom God has joined cannot be separated, and God has joined all His Sons [you, me and everybody else] with Himself." (T-8.VI.9:4)

"I [Jesus] and my Father are one with you, for you are part of Us." (T-11.I.2:5)

"This is the miracle of creation; *that it is one forever.*" (T-13.VIII.5:1)

"The only miracle that ever was is God's most holy Son, created in the one reality that is his Father." (T-13.VIII.6:5)

"He [the Holy Spirit] will surely lead you to where God and His Son await your recognition. They are joined in giving you the gift of oneness, before which all separation vanishes." (T-14.VIII.3:3-4)

"Heaven itself is union with all of creation, and with its one Creator. And Heaven remains the Will of God for you." (T-14.VIII.5:2-3)

"God's Son will always be indivisible. As we are held as one in God, so do we learn as one in Him [the Holy Spirit]. God's Teacher [the Holy Spirit] is as like to His Creator as is His Son, and through His Teacher does God proclaim His Oneness and His Son's. Listen in silence, and do not raise your voice against Him [the Holy Spirit]. For He teaches the miracle of oneness, and before His lesson division disappears. Teach like Him here, and you will remember that you have always created like your Father. The miracle of creation has never ceased, having the holy stamp of immortality upon it. This is the Will of God for all creation, and all creation joins in willing this." (T-14.XI.11:1-8)

"For God created the only relationship that has meaning, and that is His relationship with you." (T-15.VIII.6:6) Though this may appear difficult to believe here on earth, each of us is "in truth" God's one Son because we share the same eternal mind. And our eternal mind is joined 100% with God's Mind. This joining of our mind with God's is the only meaningful relationship ever created.

"Heaven is not a place nor a condition. It is merely an awareness of perfect Oneness, and the knowledge that there is nothing else; nothing outside this Oneness, and nothing else within." (T-18.VI.1:5-6)

"God's Will is One, not many. It has no opposition, for there is none beside it." (T-19.IV.A.3:5-6) There is a peace of God available to us as we study the *Course* which starts becoming understandable. As we awaken from this insane dream world and get glimpses of our real home in Heaven, we experience this peace on an increasing basis. In Lesson 107 Jesus gives us some idea of the "peace of Heaven." First he asks us to try and remember a time, even if it was less than a minute, when we were really at peace and felt loved and safe; he then asks us to imagine what it would be like to have that moment be extended to the end of time and to eternity; he then says now multiply this sense of quiet by 10,000. He concludes by telling us that having done this we have a hint, not more than the faintest intimation, of the state our mind will rest in when the "truth" has come. In conclusion, Jesus tells us that the peace we have when we're back home in Heaven is beyond anything we can possibly experience while we're still in our own dream world.

"Behold your Friend, the Christ Who stands beside you. How holy and how beautiful He is!" (T-19.IV.D.14:1-2) Taken in the context of this section of his *Course*, the "Friend" Jesus is referring to is any other person in the world whether their standing next to you or it's someone you're thinking about. Everyone "in truth" is Christ [another term for God's one Son] for the simple reason that God has but one Son. There are a few people in my life who I've had grievances (resentments) against and these are the ones who are my best teachers of the *Course*. I intellectually understand that I must see these individuals as 100% holy and beautiful and have spent a lot of time in the *Course* with the help of Jesus/Holy Spirit/Christ focusing on these few people. I know that, like me, they are Christ, God's one Son.

Following is a nice piece from Jesus which includes the oneness of Heaven: "Such is my [Jesus] will for you and your brother [that we enter Heaven together], and for each of you for one another and for himself. Here there is only holiness and joining without limit. For what is Heaven but union, direct and perfect, and without the veil of fear upon it? Here are we one, looking with perfect gentleness upon each other and on ourselves. Here all thoughts of any separation between us become impossible. You who were a prisoner in separation are now made free in Paradise. And here would I [Jesus] unite with you, my friend, my brother and my Self [God's one Son or Christ]." (T-20.III.10:1-7)

"In you is all of Heaven." (T-25.IV.5:1) Earlier, Jesus tells us that "The Kingdom of Heaven is you." This repeats this "truth." Everything God has, we have – He withholds nothing from us. Personally, I like to say "I am effectively God." I am not God, however, because there is a significant and very important difference which is that God created me and I did not create Him.

"God wills you learn what always has been true: that He created you as part of Him, and this must still be true because ideas leave not their source." (T-26.VII.13:2)

"What God calls one will be forever one, not separate. His Kingdom is united; thus it was created, and thus will it ever be." (T-26.VII.15:7-8)

"In his creation did his Father say [to his Son], 'You are beloved of Me and I of you forever. Be you perfect as Myself, for you can never be apart from Me.' His Son remembers not that he replied 'I will', though in that promise he was born." (T-28.VI.6:4-6) I talked earlier of the only relationship that is real which is the one between Us [God's one Son] and our Father. Here in this section of the *Course* Jesus tells us when this was first established in Heaven before time began.

"My mind is part of God's. I am very holy." (W-35.title) Clearly, "mind" as used here refers to the spirit part of my mind and not the ego part.

"God is in everything I see because God is in my mind. In my own mind, behind all my insane thoughts of separation and attack, is the knowledge [truth] that all is one forever. I have not lost the knowledge of Who I am [God's Son] because I have forgotten it. It has been kept for me in the Mind of God, Who has not left His Thoughts. And I, who am among them, am one with them and one with Him." (W-56.5:1-5)

"I begin to understand the holiness of all living things, including myself, and their oneness with me." (W-57.5:6)

"And as I look upon the world with the vision He has given me, I remember that I am His Son." (W-60.5:5) I often think of "vision" or "Christ's vision" as analogous to Superman's x-ray vision who can see through walls and other physical objects. Using Christ's vision, however, I don't see with my eyes at all. Rather, I simply know that this whole world of form is a mirage which my ego mind made up or as a dream which I made up and none of it is real. Mentally, I know that the "gate of Heaven" is just beyond my mirage and there's no doubt I'll be entering that gate when my dreams end. God Himself will take this final step for me when He's ready. Meanwhile, my dream world is getting happier and happier and I hope to be around here for many years to come.

"The Son of God is you." (W-64.3:4)

"*I am as God created me. I am His Son eternally.*" (W-94.3:3-4)

And to everyone else in the world who ever lived, or will be born in the future, I say along with Jesus: "*You are as God created you. You are His Son eternally.*" (W-94.5:6-7)

"*I am one Self* [Christ], *united with my Creator, at one with every aspect of creation, and limitless in power and in peace.*" (W-95.11:2) In "truth" I am effectively God and so are you but don't forget that He created us and we didn't create Him.

"You are the spirit which completes Himself, and shares His function as Creator. He is with you always, as you are with Him." (W-97.2:3-4)

"I am as God created me." (W-110.title) This is a very simple statement. It is also very important which we know because it is included as a lesson title two other times – In Lessons 94 and 162.

"I am one Self, united with my Creator. *Serenity and perfect peace are mine, because I am one Self, completely whole, at one with all creation and with God.*" (W-113.1:1-2)

"Let me remember I am one with God." (W-124.title)

"Love cannot judge. As it is one itself, it looks on all as one. Its meaning lies in oneness. And it must elude the mind that thinks of it as partial or in part. There is no love but God's, and all of love is His. There is no other principle that rules where love is not. Love is a law without an opposite. Its wholeness is the power holding everything as one, the link between the Father and the Son which holds Them both forever as the same." (W-127.3:1-8) Love, as defined here, is a synonym for Heaven which is, in "truth", the only reality. In other places, the *Course* also tells us that "God is love", "God's Son is love" and, of course, "the Holy Spirit is love"; in other words, the Holy Trinity, or Heaven, is love. Clearly when the word "love" is used in this world it seldom has anything to do with the *Course*'s definition.

"God shares His Fatherhood with you who are His Son, for He makes no distinctions in what is Himself and what is still Himself. What He creates is not apart from Him, and nowhere does the Father end, the Son begin as something separate from Him." (L-132.12:3-4)

"The power of decision is my own. This day I will accept myself as what my Father's Will created me to be." (L-152.11:3-4) Although the idea is very simple, it takes a lot of work in my experience to distinguish between the two voices in my mind – One is the ego's voice or the world's voice and the other is God's Voice. It is my decision which of these two guides I prefer to listen to. However, the happiness and joy I'm getting as a result of following God's Voice on an ever increasing basis is an endorsement for this incredible teaching guide called *A Course in Miracles.* So thank you, Jesus, as author of the *Course,* and thanks to the many people who helped bring it to fruition, beginning with Helen Schucman and William Thetford. I must also thank their young assistant, Ken Wapnick, who helped with the final editing of the *Course.* Ken also became for many years the most respected and influential student and teacher of the *Course* in the world.

"The Thought of God created you. It left you not, nor have you ever been apart from it an instant. It belongs to you. By it you live. It is your Source of [eternal] life, holding you one with it, and everything is one with you because it left you not. The Thought of God protects you, cares for you, and makes soft your resting place and smooth your way, lighting your mind with happiness and love. Eternity and everlasting life shine in your mind, because the Thought of God has left you not, and still abides with you." (W-165.2:1-7)

"Oneness is simply the idea God is. And in His Being, He encompasses all things. No mind holds anything but Him. We say 'God is,' and then we cease to speak, for in that knowledge words are meaningless. There are no lips to speak them, and no part of mind sufficiently distinct to feel that it is now aware of something not itself. It has united with its Source [our Father]. And like its Source Itself, it merely is." (L-169.5:1-7)

"God is but Love, and therefore so am I." (W-Review V.Intro.4:3)

"Now are we one with Him Who is our Source." (W-177.2:1 and W-164.title)

"It is this Child in you your Father knows as His Own Son. It is this Child Who knows His Father." (W-182.5:1-2) Child here is another name for God's one Son (or Christ) who you are and I am and so is everyone else, whether they be friend, foe or stranger to us.

"God's Name is holy, but no holier than yours. To call upon His Name is but to call upon your own." (W-183.1:1-2) This is so simply because in "truth", or in Heaven, there is but One Mind which we share with God.

"We thank our Father for one thing alone; that we are separate from no living thing, and therefore one with Him." (W-195.6:1)

"God's Name reminds me that I am His Son, not slave to time, unbound by laws which rule the world of sick illusions, free in God, forever and forever one with Him." (W-204.1:2)

"We thank You, Father, for the light that shines forever in us. And we honor it, because You share it with us. We are one, united in this light and one with You, at peace with all creation and ourselves." (W239-2:1-3)

"How far beyond this world my Self must be, and yet how near to me and close to God!" (W-252.1:5) I am God's one Son in "truth" and so are you. Jesus uses the word "Self", with a capital "S", to define this shared identity with each other so "Son of God" and "Christ" and "Self" are all synonyms. Not only are we close to God but we have everything that He has because He and We, His Son, are one.

"Let me forget my brother's past today." (W-288.title) *"This is the thought that leads the way to You, and brings me to my goal. I cannot come to You without my brother. And to know my Source [our Father], I first must recognize what You created one with me. My brother's is the hand that leads me on the way to You." (W-288.1:1-4)*

"Creation is the sum of all God's Thoughts, in number infinite, and everywhere without all limit. Only love creates, and only like itself. There was no time when all that it created was not there [though this idea is completely screened out while we believe this world is real]. Nor will there be a time when anything that it created suffers any loss. Forever and forever are God's Thoughts exactly as they were and as they are, unchanged through time and after time is done." (W-Q 11.1:1-5)

"Creation is the opposite of all illusions, for creation is the truth." (W-Q 11.3:1) The term "all illusions" refers to every aspect of this world of time and space and separate forms with its birth and death, happy times and suffering, blame and guilt, etc. Creation is the extension of Heaven, which is completely opposite to this insane world, and Creation is the "truth."

"Let me not forget myself is nothing, but my Self is all." (W-358.1:7) This literally tells me that Jimmy Laws is "nothing" whereas my true identity as Christ, God's one Son ["my Self"] is "everything". Generally, this seems to be about the most difficult of the ego's tricks to overcome. The ego will likely tell you that you'll lose your individual identity and be absorbed into some "blob." However, it's been my experience that with continued mind training using Jesus' *Course*, any arguments the ego continues to throw my way are easily dismissed. One simple thought helps me in this regard: Emotionally, do I want to go through all the ups and downs this world throws my way with death my "final reward" or would I rather feel happy, joyous and free for all eternity and be effectively God? I've chosen the second choice.

"Unity alone is not a thing of dreams. And it is this God's teachers acknowledge as behind the dream, beyond all seeming and yet surely theirs." (M-12.6:10-11)

"The Will of God is One and all there is. This is your heritage. The universe [Heaven] beyond the sun and stars, and all the thoughts of which you can conceive, belongs to you. God's peace is the condition for His Will. Attain His peace, and you remember Him." (M-20.6:9-13)

"As God created you [His one Son or Christ], you *have* all power. The image you made of yourself [the son of man or Jimmy Laws in my case] has none." (M-29.4:4-5)

"This Will [Our's and God's combined] is always unified and therefore has no meaning in this world. It has no opposite and no degrees." (C-1.4:4-5)

"God does not know of separation. What He knows is only that He has one Son." (Psy-2.VII.1:11-12)

"What God created one must recognize its oneness, and rejoice that what illusions seemed to separate [i.e., the world] is one forever in the Mind of God." (Song-1.Intro.2:3)

"To ask that Christ be but Himself is not an entreaty [i.e., it's not a real request]. It is a song of thanksgiving for what you are." (Song-1.I.7:2-3)

"Let it never be forgotten that prayer at any level is always for yourself." (Song-1.II.6:1) The reason is obvious – Each and every one of us is Christ, God's one Son. So if I pray for anyone, I am praying for Christ Who I am too.

"Illusions are untrue. [And this whole world is an illusion.] God's Will is truth, and you are one with Him in Will and purpose [forever]. Here all dreams are done." (Song-2.III.4:7-9) Jesus emphasizes the fact that the world is an illusion (or a dream) and is not at all real in Lesson 132 of the Workbook for Students. Specifically he states: "There is no world! This is the central thought the course attempts to teach." (W-132.6:2-3)

Chapter 5: Listen to Jesus and not to the ego

This chapter consists of 2 sections as follows:

Section A: Overview

As Jesus points out in *A Course in Miracles* (the *Course*), the purpose of the *Course* is to train our minds to listen to the Voice for God and not to listen to the voice of the ego. The Voice for God can be thought of as the Voice of Jesus, the Holy Spirit, or Christ since they are one. For me personally, I think of God's Voice as coming from Jesus because, like me, he was a person stuck in this dream world. I also definitely think of Jesus as my best friend because he always knows what's best for me.

The ego's voice is the voice for the world and its continuation. It is analogous to the voice of Satan or the devil in Biblical terminology.

It is very clear that when we have disciplined our minds to only listen to the Voice for God, we have achieved the goal of the *Course*. Once this has occurred we are considered to be in the "real world" in the terminology of the *Course*. Personally, I have made a lot of progress to this end but I have not reached the "real world" yet.

Through the mind training of the *Course*, we learn to adhere on an increasing basis to the Voice for God and to disregard the ego's voice. The result is that our fears are reduced as we progress and we easily comprehend that death is not a reality for anyone because God created us as eternal joyful parts of His Creation. Other good students of the *Course* will agree that this crazy insane dream world becomes an extremely happy place to be in as we make progress in accomplishing the *Course*'s mind training goal for us.

Over the 18 years that I have been studying the *Course*, it has become much easier for me to listen on an increasing basis to Jesus and to disregard the ego.

Section B: Specific references to listening for Jesus

The purpose of this section is to point out some of the places in the *Course* where Jesus talks about this objective of listening to him (or the Holy Spirit or Christ) rather than the ego for guidance.

All of us human beings here on earth have two parts to our minds. We have the permanent eternal part of our mind which Jesus refers to as our spirit mind. And then we have our ego mind which believes that this world is real and pain and suffering and death are our lot and establishes an ongoing fear within us so long as we listen to it.

Following are some of the sections in the *Course* where Jesus makes a distinction between these two parts of our mind and teaches us to stop listening to the ego and start listening only to the Voice for God (the Voice of Jesus/the Holy Spirit/Christ):

"The ego is afraid of the spirit's joy, because once you have experienced it you will withdraw all protection from the ego, and become totally without investment in fear. Your investment is great now because fear is a witness to the separation, and your ego rejoices when you witness to it. Leave it behind! Do not listen to it and do not preserve it. Listen only to God, Who is as incapable of deception as is the spirit He created." (T-4.I.10:1-5)

"Your mind and mine can unite in shining your ego away, releasing the strength of God into everything you think and do." (T-4.IV.8:3) This is a wonderful promise from Jesus. He literally tells us that when we join our minds with his, we shine the ego away leaving us with God's strength in all we think and do. Thank you Jesus!

"When the ego was made, God placed in the mind the Call to joy. This Call is so strong that the ego always dissolves at Its sound. That is why you must choose to hear one of two voices within you. One you made yourself, and that one is not of God. But the other is given you by God, Who asks you only to listen to it. The Holy Spirit is in you in a very literal sense. His is the Voice that calls you back to where you were before [i.e., Heaven] and will be again. It is possible even in this world to hear only that Voice and no other. It takes effort and great willingness to learn. It is the final lesson that I learned, and God's Sons are as equal as learners as they are as Sons." (T-5.II.3:2-11) Here is where Jesus tells us that he was able to hear only the Voice for God. Additionally, he tells us that if he could do it, so can we. Also, please note from the first sentence of this quote that another term Jesus uses for the Holy Spirit is "the Call to joy."

"Obey the Holy Spirit, and you will be giving up the ego. But you will be sacrificing nothing. On the contrary, you will be gaining everything. If you believed this, there would be no conflict." (T-7.X.3:8-10)

"There is a rationale for choice. Only one Teacher knows what your reality is. If learning to remove the obstacles to that knowledge is the purpose of the curriculum, you must learn it of Him." (T-8.II.1:1-3) The purpose of the *Course* is, of course, to learn to remove the obstacles that prevent us from knowing our own reality. The words "Teacher" in the 2nd sentence and "Him" in the 3rd sentence are references to the Holy Spirit.

"On this journey you have chosen me [Jesus] as your companion *instead* of the ego. Do not attempt to hold on to both, or you will try to go in different directions and will lose the way." (T-8.V.5:8-9) About 2,000 years ago, Jesus told us the same thing: "You can't serve two masters."

"Think like Him [the Holy Spirit] ever so slightly, and the little spark becomes a blazing light that fills your mind so that He becomes your only Guest. Whenever you ask the ego to enter, you lessen His welcome. He will remain, but you have allied yourself against Him. Whatever journey you choose to take, He will go with you, waiting. You can safely trust His patience, for He cannot leave a part of God." (T-11.II.5:4-8)

"Do you realize that the ego must set you on a journey which cannot but lead to a sense of futility and depression? To seek and not to find is hardly joyous. Is this the promise you would keep? The Holy Spirit offers you another promise, and one that will lead to joy. For His promise is 'Seek and you *will* find,' and under His guidance you cannot be defeated." (T-12.IV.4:1-5)

"Each day, each hour and minute, even each second, you are deciding between the crucifixion and the resurrection; between the ego and the Holy Spirit. The ego is the choice for guilt; the Holy Spirit the choice for guiltlessness [i.e., innocence]. The power of decision is all that is yours. What you can decide between is fixed, because there are no alternatives except truth and illusion. And there is no overlap between them, because they are opposites which cannot be reconciled and cannot both be true. You are guilty or guiltless, bound or free, unhappy or happy." (T-14.III.4:1-6)

"Call not upon the ego for anything; it is only this that you need do. The Holy Spirit will, of Himself, fill every mind that so makes room for Him. If you want peace you must abandon the teacher of attack [i.e., the ego]." (T-14.XI.13:5-6)

"You cannot be faithful to two masters who ask conflicting things of you." (T-17.I.2:4)

This quote expands somewhat on not being able to serve two masters – "Perception cannot obey two masters, each asking for messages of different things in different languages." (T-19.IV.A.11:3)

The following tells us why it's not a good idea to listen to the ego: "Listen to what the ego says, and see what it directs you see, and it is sure that you will see yourself as tiny, vulnerable and afraid. You will experience depression, a sense of worthlessness, and feelings of impermanence and unreality. You will believe that you are helpless prey to forces far beyond your own control, and far more powerful than you. And you will think the world you made directs your destiny. For this will be your faith. But never believe because it is your faith it makes reality." [i.e., Faith in the ego and the ego's version of "God" is faith in illusion rather than reality.] (T-21.V.2:3-8)

"There are two teachers only, who point in different ways. And you will go along the way your chosen teacher leads." (T-26.V.1:7-8)

"The ego does constant battle with the Holy Spirit on the fundamental question of what your function is. So does it do constant battle with the Holy Spirit about what your happiness is. It is not a two-way battle. The ego attacks and the Holy Spirit does not respond. He knows what your function is. He knows it is your happiness." (W-66.2:1-6) As I've advanced over the years I've been studying the *Course*, I am responding much less to ego thoughts whether they appear to be coming from me or from others and I am becoming happier beyond anything I could have imagined 18 years ago when I first started the *Course*.

"We have seen that there are only two parts of your mind. One is ruled by the ego, and is made up of illusions. The other is the home of the Holy Spirit, where truth abides. There are no other guides but these to choose between, and no other outcomes possible as a result of your choice but the fear that the ego always engenders, and the love that the Holy Spirit always offers to replace it." (W-66.7:2-5) So I have only 2 choices within my mind – If I choose the Voice for God as my guide I'll know love but if I choose the ego as my guide I'll know fear. The idea is simple but it's not easy and it takes time in my experience.

Regarding the ego, this quote is "Hear not its voice." (W-151.6:1)

"I will step back and let Him [the Holy Spirit] lead the way." (W-155.title)

"*I hear the Voice that God has given me, and it is only this my mind obeys.*" (W-199.8:9)

"Let every voice but God's be still in me." (W-254.title)

"Today we let no ego thoughts direct our words or actions. When such thoughts occur, we quietly step back and look at them, and then we let them go. We do not want what they would bring with them. And so we do not choose to keep them. They are silent now. And in the stillness, hallowed by His Love, God speaks to us and tells us of our will, as we have chosen to remember Him." (W-254.2:1-6)

"In this world the only remaining freedom is the freedom of choice; always between two choices or two voices." [i.e., the Voice for God leading to love or the voice of the ego leading to fear.] (C-1.7:1)

Chapter 6: Spiritual progress

This chapter consists of 2 sections as follows:

Section A: Overview

The *Course* never uses the term "spiritual progress". It is a term that I use to describe the ever increasing use of the Voice for God to be my mind's guide and the ever decreasing use of the ego as my guide. The result for me, of course, is an ever increasing happiness in all my (dream) worldly affairs and relationships. Other long term students of the *Course*, I'm sure, will be able to identify with this beautiful evolution of our lives.

Although Jesus does not use the term "spiritual progress", he makes reference to the idea many times. The primary purpose of this chapter is to point some of these out.

The reason I have included this chapter in this book is to encourage new *Course* students to make the *Course* more than a onetime study to be set aside once completed. The best way I can do this is by sharing my own experience. By the early part of 2000, I had completed the 3 books of the *Course*, and I knew that I had benefitted from them. There is nothing in the *Course* itself that suggests it should or need be repeated. However, within two or three months of completing the *Course* that first time, I decided to start the *Course* again – I studied the Text, did the 365 Lessons and studied the Manual for Teachers so by around the middle of 2001 I had concluded my second go round of this amazing spiritual material. One thing I noticed is that, although I had been through the same material before, it was very much as if it was all brand new to me. It was also easier the second time around. Of more importance was that my level of happiness and contentment was improved significantly. Today, after many more rounds in the *Course*, I expect to continue my *Course* studies for the rest of my life here and continue making "spiritual progress."

Section B: Specific references to spiritual progress

Following are some quotes from *A Course in Miracles* (the *Course*) regarding spiritual progress:

"You have very little trust in me [Jesus] as yet, but it will increase as you turn more and more often to me instead of to your ego for guidance." (T-4.VI.3:1)

"If you will accept only what is timeless as real, you will begin to understand eternity and make it yours." (T-10.V.14:9) The beginning of spiritual progress is when we start understanding that what God created is, like Himself, eternal or timeless and nothing else is real. Nothing here on earth is eternal which means nothing here is real. The following are physical in nature, are not real and are not eternal (they will end): Our bodies, planet earth, the sun and moon, all other planets and far away galaxies, black holes, etc. The *Course*'s general term for such things is "illusions" (or "dreams").

"The Guest Whom God sent you [the Holy Spirit] will teach you how to do this [i.e., be like God], if you but recognize the little spark and are willing to let it grow. Your willingness need not be perfect, because His is. If you will merely offer Him a little place, He will lighten it so much that you will gladly let it be increased. And by this increase, you will begin to remember creation [Heaven]." (T-11.II.6:5-8)

"As you perceive more and more common elements in all situations, the transfer of training under the Holy Spirit's guidance increases and becomes generalized. Gradually you learn to apply it to everyone and everything, for its applicability is universal." (T-12.VI.6:5-6)

"Yet as I [Jesus] become more real to you, you will learn that you do want only that." (T-12.VII.11:5) The last word, "that," in this quote refers to the acceptance of my mission to extend peace which means I will find peace.

"You will first dream of peace, and then awaken to it." (T-13.VII.9:1)

"Unite with me [Jesus] under the holy banner of His [the Holy Spirit's] teaching, and as we grow in strength the power of God's Son will move in us, and we will leave no one untouched and no one left alone." (T-13.VIII.8:2)

"The Holy Spirit will teach you how to use it [God's peace], and by extending it, to learn that it is in you." (T-13.XI.8:6)

"You will learn salvation because you will learn how to save." (T-13.XI.9:1)

"This is an insane world, and do not underestimate the extent of its insanity. There is no area of your perception that it has not touched and your dream *is* sacred to you. That is why God placed the Holy Spirit in you, where you placed the dream." (T-14.I.2:6-8) Every child ever born into this world initially believed this world was absolutely real and this, of course, includes Jesus. This is our common starting point before any spiritual progress has occurred. The simple truth, however, is God creates only the eternal and only what God creates is real. Since neither this world nor anything in it is eternal, none of it is real. It's all a dream or an illusion.

"The Holy Spirit, therefore, must begin His teaching by showing you what you can never learn [without His help]." (T-14.I.5:1)

"You who have not yet brought all of the darkness you have taught yourself into the light in you, can hardly judge the truth and value of this course." (T-14.XI.4:1) This was certainly true for me when I first read this sentence about 18 years ago. The *Course* explicitly states that its goal for us is peace and happiness. The ongoing study of the *Course* for me since then has proven that it is accomplishing its goal way beyond my wildest expectations *on an increasing basis*. I therefore plan on studying it for the rest of my life.

"The Holy Spirit leads as steadily to Heaven as the ego drives to hell." (T-15.I.7:4) Note that Jesus tells us quite succinctly here that if we're not making spiritual progress then we're heading towards hell.

"For a time you may attempt to bring illusions into the holy instant, to hinder your full awareness of the complete difference, in all respects, between your experience of truth and illusion. Yet you will not attempt this long. In the holy instant the power of the Holy Spirit will prevail, because you joined Him." (T-16.VII.7:1-3)

"And with each step in His [the Holy Spirit's] undoing is the separation more and more undone, and union brought closer." (T-17.III.6:4)

"I [Jesus] hold your hand as surely as you agreed to take your brother's. You will not separate, for I stand with you and walk with you in your advance to truth. And where we go we carry God with us." (T-18.III.5:5-7)

"Heaven is joined with you in your advance to Heaven." (T-18.III.8:3)

Please note the promises included in these lines from the *Course* which have been unfolding in my life for the past 18 years that I've been studying the *Course*: "As peace extends from deep inside yourself to embrace all the Sonship and give it rest, it will encounter many obstacles. Some of them you will try to impose. Others will seem to arise from elsewhere; from your brothers, and from various aspects of the world outside. Yet peace will gently cover them, extending past completely unencumbered. The extension of the Holy Spirit's purpose from your relationship to others, to bring them gently in, is the way in which He will bring means and goal in line. The peace He lay, deep within you and your brother, will quietly extend to every aspect of your life, surrounding you and your brother with glowing happiness and the calm awareness of complete protection. And you will carry its message of love and freedom to everyone who draws nigh unto your temple, where healing waits for him. You will not wait to give him this, for you will call to him and he will answer you, recognizing in your call the Call for God. And you will draw him in and give him rest, as it was given you." (T-19.IV.1:1-9)

When we start studying the *Course* the beginning of our spiritual progress is well defined in the following paragraph: "The fear of death will go as its appeal is yielded to love's real attraction. The end of sin, which nestles quietly in the safety of your relationship, protected by your union with your brother, and ready to grow into a mighty force for God is very near. The infancy of salvation is carefully guarded by love, preserved from every thought that would attack it, and quietly made ready to fulfill the mighty task for which it was given you. Your newborn purpose is nursed by angels, cherished by the Holy Spirit and protected by God Himself. It needs not your protection; it is *yours*. For it is deathless, and within it lies the end of death." (T-19.IV.C.9:1-6)

"Vision will come to you at first in glimpses; but they will be enough to show you what is given you who see your brother sinless." (T-20.VIII.1:1)

When we begin our spiritual progress, Jesus tells us: "Not wholly mad, you have been willing to look on much of your insanity and recognize its madness. Your faith is moving inward, past insanity and on to reason." (T-21.IV.4:2-3)

As a fairly advanced student of the *Course*, the following still holds true for me: "At times it |i.e., the ego| still deceives you. Yet in your saner moments, its ranting strikes no terror in your heart. For you have realized that all the gifts it would withdraw from you, in rage at your 'presumptuous' wish to look within, you do not want. A few remaining trinkets still seem to shine and catch your eye. Yet you would not 'sell' Heaven to have them." (T-21.IV.6:4-8)

"For reason, kind as is the purpose for which it is the means, leads steadily away from madness toward the goal of truth." (T-21.VI.7:10)

"This course makes no attempt to teach what cannot easily be learned. Its scope does not exceed your own, except to say that what is yours will come to you when you are ready." (T-24.VII.8:1-2) It can be said that the whole purpose of the *Course* is to change our internal teacher from the ego to the Holy Spirit (or Jesus or Christ) and this shift begins when we start our studying. What this sentence says is that our actual future learning will be given us by the Holy Spirit when we are ready for it; it is not up to us, except to prepare ourselves for it.

"To each his special function is designed to be perceived as possible, and more and more desired, as it proves to him that it is an alternative he really wants." (T-25.VII.9:2)

Regarding this dream world which I'm still in and so are you, Jesus tells us: "In the dreams He |the Holy Spirit| brings there is no murder and there is no death. The dream of guilt |and blame| is fading from your sight, although your eyes are closed. A smile has come to lighten up your sleeping face. The sleep is peaceful now, for these are happy dreams." (T-27.VII.14:5-8)

"Here does the dream of separation start to fade and disappear." (T-30.IV.8:1)

"Thus are the Holy Spirit's lesson plans arranged in easy steps, that though there be some lack of ease at times and some distress, there is no shattering of what was learned, but just a re-translation of what seems to be the evidence on its behalf." (T-31.V.9:1)

"All that is given you is for release; the sight, the vision and the inner Guide all lead you out of hell with those you love beside you, and the universe with them." (T-31.VII.7:7)

"As forgiveness allows love to return to my awareness, I will see a world of peace and safety and joy." (W-55.3:4)

"Do not forget how little you have learned. Do not forget how much you can learn now. Do not forget your Father's need of you, as you review these thoughts He gave to you." (W-Review III.Intro.13:1-4)

"Not everyone is ready to accept it [That 'There is no world!' because it's all just a dream and not at all real.], and each one must go as far as he can let himself be led along the road to truth. He will return and go still farther, or perhaps step back a while and then return again." (W-132.6:4-5)

"Between these paths [both of which believe the world is real] there is another road that leads away from loss of every kind, for sacrifice and deprivation both are quickly left behind. This is the way appointed for you now." (W-155.5:1-2)

"And we step forth toward this [Heaven], as we progress along the way that truth points out to us." (W-155.11:3)

The next 3 quote sections represent the first 3 paragraphs from the Introduction to Review V (which is right after Lesson 170 of the Workbook). Individually and collectively they do a great job in telling us of spiritual progress yet to be made.

> "We now review again. This time we are ready to give more effort and more time to what we undertake. We recognize we are preparing for another phase of understanding. We would take this step completely, that we may go on again more certain, more

sincere, with faith upheld more surely. Our footsteps have not been unwavering, and doubts have made us walk uncertainly and slowly on the road this course sets forth. But now we hasten on, for we approach a greater certainty, a firmer purpose and a surer goal." (W-Review V.Intro.1:1-6)

"Steady our feet, our Father. Let our doubts be quiet and our holy minds be still, and speak to us. We have no words to give to you. We would but listen to Your Word, and make it ours. Lead our practicing as does a father lead a little child along a way he does not understand. Yet does he follow, sure that he is safe because his father leads the way for him." (W-Review V.Intro.2:1-6)

"So do we bring our practicing to You. And if we stumble, You will raise us up. If we forget the way, we count upon Your sure remembering. We wander off, but You will not forget to call us back. Quicken our footsteps now, that we may walk more certainly and quickly unto You. And we accept the Word You offer us to unify our practicing, as we review the thoughts that You have given us." (W-Review V.Intro.3:1-6)

"And it is this [eternal union with our Father and His Creation] that waits to meet us at the journey's ending. Every step we take brings us a little nearer." (W-Review V.Intro.5:1-2)

"Our next few lessons make a special point of firming up your willingness to make your weak commitment strong; your scattered goals blend into one intent." (W-Introduction to Lessons 181-200.1:1)

"Step back from fear, and make advance to love." (W-196.11:6)

"The stillness of today will give us hope that we have found the way, and travelled far along it to a wholly certain goal [Heaven]." (W-286.2:1)

"Father, our eyes are opening at last." (W-302.1:1)

"This is the faith that will endure, and take me farther and still farther on the road that leads to Him." (W-327.1:4)

"Yet it [a miracle] paves the way for the return of timelessness and love's awakening, for fear must slip away under the gentle remedy it brings." (W-Q 13.1:6)

"Faithfulness is the teacher of God's trust in the Word of God to set all things right; not some, but all. Generally, his faithfulness begins by resting on just some problems, remaining carefully limited for a time. To give up all problems to one Answer [the Holy Spirit] is to reverse the thinking of the world entirely. And that alone is faithfulness. Nothing but that really deserves the name. Yet each degree, however small, is worth achieving. Readiness, as the text notes, is not mastery." (M-4.IX.1:4-10)

"There are those who are called upon to change their life situation almost immediately, but these are generally special cases. By far the majority are given a slowly evolving training program, in which as many previous mistakes as possible are corrected. Relationships in particular must be properly perceived, and all dark cornerstones of unforgiveness removed. Otherwise the old thought system still has a basis for return." (M-9.1:6-9)

The following paragraph not only talks of spiritual progress but it also explains how the *Course*'s thought system is completely opposite to the world's thought system. "As the teacher of God advances in his training, he learns one lesson with increasing thoroughness. He does not make his own decisions; he asks his Teacher (Jesus/Holy Spirit/Christ) for His answer, and it is this he follows as his guide for action. This becomes easier and easier, as the teacher of God learns to give up his own judgment. The giving up of judgment, the obvious prerequisite for hearing God's Voice, is usually a fairly slow process, not because it is difficult, but because it is apt to be perceived as personally insulting. The world's training is directed toward achieving a goal in direct opposition to that of our curriculum. The world trains for reliance on one's judgment as the criterion for maturity and strength. Our curriculum trains for the relinquishment of judgment as the necessary condition of salvation." (M-9.2:1-7)

"The progress of the teacher of God may be slow or rapid, depending on whether he recognizes the Atonement's inclusiveness, or for a time excludes some problem areas from it. In some cases, there is a sudden and complete awareness of the perfect applicability of the lesson of the Atonement to all situations, but this is comparatively rare. The teacher of God may have accepted the function God has given him long before he has learned all that his acceptance holds out to him. It is only the end that is certain [Heaven]. Anywhere along the way, the necessary realization of inclusiveness may reach him. If the way seems long, let him be content. He has decided on the direction he wants to take. What more was asked of him? And having done what was required, would God withhold the rest? [Answer: Of course not!]" (M-22.2:1-9)

"Do not despair, then, because of limitations. It is your function to escape from them, but not to be without them. If you would be heard by those who suffer, you must speak their language. If you would be a savior, you must understand what needs to be escaped. Salvation is not theoretical. Behold the problem, ask for the answer, and then accept it when it comes. Nor will its coming be long delayed. All the help you can accept will be provided, and not one need you have will not be met. Let us not, then, be too concerned with goals for which you are not ready. God takes you where you are and welcomes you. What more could you desire, when this is all you need?" (M-26.4:1-11)

"There is another advantage, – and a very important one, – in referring decisions to the Holy Spirit with increasing frequency." (M-29.3:1)

"At its highest it [i.e., awareness] becomes aware of the real world, and can be trained to do so increasingly." (C.1.7:5)

"Faith in your goal [Heaven] will grow and hold you up as you ascend the shining stairway to the lawns of Heaven and the gate of peace." (Song.1.Intro.3:3)

The *Song of Prayer* pamphlet contains 3 chapters – Prayer, Forgiveness and Healing. Section II of the Prayer chapter is entitled "The Ladder of Prayer" and is approximately 2 pages long. As this title indicates, it talks about spiritual progress in our prayer life from the bottom rungs of the ladder to the top rung which is often referred to in the *Course* as the "gate of Heaven." I have not copied these 2 pages here but I encourage you to read them at this time.

Chapter 7: My long memorized meditation

This chapter consists of 2 sections as follows:

Section A: Overview ..... Contained on this page.

Section B: My long memorized meditation ..... page 66.

Section A: Overview

Quite a few years ago I developed a personal long meditation which largely summarizes the *Course*. It has changed and evolved over the years and will no doubt change in the future. I mentally say it at least once a day, usually towards the end of the day.

Although there is nothing in the *Course* which suggests this procedure, I have found it to be a powerful tool towards improving my spiritual progress. As a result of my experience, other *Course* students might consider establishing their own personal daily memorized meditation.

Section B, which follows, reflects this meditation as it stands today. Please note that the words contained in brackets ([   ]) are not included in my meditation words but will help you understand my thinking underlying the words. Also note that where I have a break between groups of sentences it is because I think of the new group of sentences as a new set of ideas from the preceding group.

Section B: My long memorized meditation

"I am not a body. I am free. For I am still as God created me."

"Your answer is some form of peace – All pain is healed; all misery replaced with joy; all prison doors are opened; and all sin is understood as merely a mistake."

"Forgiveness ends the dream of conflict here." [Jesus tells us in the *Course* that conflict is the root of all evil. 100% forgiveness all the time means we have attained the real world, our ultimate goal while we're here in our dream world.]

"I am not a body. I am free. For I am still as God created me." [Remember God created but One Son. You are that One Son as is Jesus, me and everyone else.]

"I hear the Voice that You have given me and it is only This my mind obeys." [This is our ultimate goal here – to only follow God's Voice and never the ego's voice. When this is achieved we have attained the real world which also means we have complete (100%) forgiveness.]

"No one can fail who seeks to reach the Truth."

"I will step back and let You lead the way, Jesus/Holy Spirit/Christ, because I want to be happy. [And They say something like:] 'And this is what We want for you too Jimmy.'"

"Forgiveness is the home of miracles."

"What's a miracle? I question the illusion and I get the right answer – I made this whole world up." [Wherever I'm at, I often open my eyes and look around me and whatever I see or hear I do my best to understand it's all just a dream coming from my mind.] "I correct it or replace it with a Holy Instant. I'm willing to give up all my littleness; I'm humble before God but great in Him; I forget the future; and I say: 'This Holy Instant would I give to you, Jesus. Be you in charge for I would follow you, certain that your direction gives me peace.'"

"Now I'm in the Holy Instant room with just me and Jesus and I say: 'God grant me peace' and then we [Jesus and I] go quietly into the Holy Spirit and I say 'My only decision is for Heaven.'". [The Holy Instant room is something I made up to represent a private room in my mind with only Jesus and I there before we move on to the Holy Spirit and then Christ and then to God Himself.]

"Now I [and Jesus and the Holy Spirit] go into Christ and I know We [all of God's Creation] are all One."

"And then I [as Christ] go into the Father and I say: 'I'm immersed in Your Love, surrounded by Your Love and I am Your Love. Peace, light and joy are mine. You [Father] are the donut and We [Christ] are the hole [I think of a physical donut and separately a donut hole which most donut shops also sell. When the donut hole is pushed into the center of the donut, it is fully protected by the donut just as God protects us all.] - safe and sound [the cliché that means 'all is well'] and sure [there are no decisions in Heaven, only certainty], sane and serene now and forever and ever and ever. Above the battleground, I am determined to join with you, Jesus. Thus, I am Christ, the same as you.' Jesus tells me: 'Let's go straight to the gate of Heaven and look both ways.' I first look at Heaven and see only eternal peace. [At this point in my meditation, my mind is in the 'Holy Instant' mode, a term which Jesus defines in his *Course*.] Then, without using my eyes, I look at the world knowing it's all illusion especially the body and life of Jimmy Laws [I accept Atonement for myself]."

"Forgiveness is the only gift we give."

"God is in everything I 'see' because God is in my mind." [At this point, I often glance around me and do my best to use vision and know that Heaven is right behind my illusionary world.]

"Peace to us [Jesus and I], the Holy Son of God. Peace to our brothers who are one with us. Let all the world be blessed with peace through us."

"If I defend myself, I am attacked. Today I will make no decisions for myself but I'll step back and let You lead the way, Jesus/Holy Spirit/Christ, because I want to be happy and I know that's what You want for me. [And They say something like:] 'That's a really good idea Jimmy.'"

"Our [me, Jesus/Holy Spirit/Christ] happy holiness blesses the world. We use constant vision now."

"I am not a body. I am free for I'm still as God created me." [At this point, I state whatever lesson I'm working on for the day so if I'm doing Lesson 48 I'd say 'There is nothing to fear.'] "I am not a body. I am free for I'm still as God created me."

"Don't judge but use Christ's Vision instead. You [Literally this refers to every other individual in the world. If I have some grievance against someone, then that person often comes to my mind at this point in my meditation.] and I and God are one. You are spirit, whole and innocent. All is forgiven and released. I honor you because of Who you are which is Christ, the same as me."

"I join with everything I think: peace, light, joy, happiness, laughter, freedom and gratitude. Peace, light and joy. And I say: 'You [Father] are the donut and We [Christ] are the hole – safe and sound and sure, sane and serene now and forever and ever and ever. Above the battleground, I am determined to join with you, Jesus. Thus, I am Christ, the same as you.' Jesus tells me: 'Let's go straight to the gate of Heaven and look both ways.' I first look at Heaven and see only eternal peace. [Another 'Holy Instant.'] Then, without using my eyes, I look at the world knowing it's all illusion especially the body and life of Jimmy Laws [I accept Atonement for myself]."

"And I join with everything in the world because God is in everything I 'see' because God is in my mind. [Again, I often look around me at this point, use vision, and know that Heaven is just on the other side of my worldly illusions.] And I use the power of the light of forgiveness, which means the same as Atonement, healing, salvation and true perception, which says the world never happened because the separation never happened but while I'm in this insane dream that I made up, I'll step back and let You lead the way, Jesus/Holy

Spirit/Christ. Thank You, Father, and of course thank You Jesus, Holy Spirit and Christ also."

"Forgiveness is the key to happiness! Forgiveness offers everything I want! I accept forgiveness for myself and say: 'God is. God is. God is and the world is not. Peace, light, joy, happiness, laughter, freedom and gratitude. Peace, light and joy. You are the donut, Father, and We are the hole. We are safe and sound and sure, sane and serene now and forever and ever and ever. Above the battleground, I am determined to join with you, Jesus. Thus, I am Christ, the same as you.' Jesus tells me: 'Let's go straight to the gate of Heaven and look both ways.' I first look at Heaven and see only eternal peace. ['Holy Instant' number 3.] Then, without using my eyes, I look at the world knowing it's all illusion especially the body and life of Jimmy Laws [I accept Atonement for myself]."

"But while I'm in this insane dream that I made up, I'll step back and let You lead the way, Jesus/Holy Spirit/Christ, because I want to be happy. [And They say something like:] 'That's a real good idea because that's what We want for you too Jimmy.'"

"I came for the salvation of the world."

"I am affected only by my thoughts."

"My sinless brothers are my guide to peace and my sinful brothers are my guide to pain, and which I choose to see I will behold."

"Peace to us [Jesus and me], the Holy Son of God and peace to our brothers who are one with us. Let all the world be blessed with peace through us."

"If I defend myself, I am attacked. Today, I will make no decisions for myself but will step back and let You lead the way, Jesus/Holy Spirit/Christ, because I want to be happy. [And They say something like:] 'A real good idea because that's what We want for you too Jimmy.'"

"My present happiness is all I see. All fear is passed and only love is here."

"The Holy Spirit speaks through us today – Jesus and me."

"Let me not see myself as limited. Let me not see anyone else as limited. Let me perceive no differences today. Our Father and all life are one. That's why:

> Jesus says 'No one is a body and there are no forms for they are one with us.'

> The Holy Spirit says 'No one is a body and there are no forms because they are one with you guys (Jesus and me) and you guys are one with Me.'

> And our Father knows that no one is a body and there are no forms for He never created any bodies or forms and He and we [all people] and the Holy Spirit are one."

"Be passersby. Be gentle. Be kind. Be generous. Be Love." [The expression 'be passersby' to me means accept the whole world as a dream, don't take it seriously and just 'pass it by.']

"Only hold onto eternal loving thoughts. When I have unloving thoughts, I will forgive and they will disappear."

"Let go of all grievances or resentments. You [reference to every person in the world, especially for those I have some grievance against] and I and God are one. You are spirit, whole and innocent. All is forgiven and released. I honor you because of who you are, which is Christ, the same as me."

"Don't attack. Forgive."

"[God says to me:] 'You made it all up anyway, Jimmy.'" [God here means the Voice for God.]

"I am real because the world is not [real]."

"Thank You, Father, for all Your gifts to me."

"[And God says:] 'You're welcome. Now see only One Spirit because that's all there is.'" [Again, God here means the Voice for God.]

"But while I'm in this insane dream that I made up, I'll step back and let you lead the way, Jesus/Holy Spirit/Christ, because I want to be happy. [And They say something like:] 'That's a real good idea because that's what We want for you too, Jimmy.'"

"I am not a body. I am free for I'm still as God created me. [At this point, I state again whatever lesson I'm working on for the day so if I'm doing Lesson 48 I'd say 'There is nothing to fear'.] I am not a body. I am free for I'm still as God created me."

Note: During the course of my waking hours, I go to a 'Holy Instant' many times. Usually, this is a quick version as follows:

"Sane and serene now and forever and ever and ever. Above the battleground, I am determined to join with you, Jesus. Thus, I am Christ, the same as you. Jesus tells me: 'Let's go straight to the gate of Heaven and look both ways.' I first look at Heaven and see only eternal peace. [Now I'm in a 'Holy Instant.'] Then, without using my eyes, I look at the world knowing it's all illusion especially the body and life of Jimmy Laws [I accept Atonement for myself]."

Part II: Ken Wapnick

Introduction

For four decades Ken Wapnick taught *A Course in Miracles* (the *Course*) to students from all over the world. It was for only his last two years that I got to know this remarkable man - from the spring of 2011, when I attended one of his multiple day workshops, until a few months after the spring of 2013, when I attended my last workshop with him. I attended a total of four workshops during the two year period that I knew Ken. Ken became ill shortly after I had lunch with him in the spring of 2013 and passed away in December of 2013.

During the two year period that I knew Ken, he became my spiritual mentor and one of my best friends I've ever had in my life. Although our mutual love for the *Course* was the foundation for our relationship, our personalities meshed wonderfully. If you read our correspondence contained in this section, you will get an excellent picture of our friendship. You should also recognize how he cheerfully guided me ever further into the thought system suggested by Jesus in his *Course*. Although once in a while Ken and I talked by phone, these were always brief conversations. Nearly our entire personal relationship is contained in the "pen pal" letters contained in this "Part II" section of this book.

I want to describe an incident that occurred during the last workshop I attended (in the spring of 2013) which told me how much Ken truly must have loved me. For those of you who have never attended any of Ken's workshops in Temecula, California, I'll describe the scene. In the teaching room, there were seats for approximately 250 attendees with very few empty seats. As was his habit, Ken would have a break after about 1-1/2 hours of teaching. During the break, a whole bunch of us would mill about the lobby, others would step outside into the California day and some would stay in the teaching room. Meanwhile, Ken would circulate around saying hi to his many friends. Now for the incident! During one of these breaks, I was talking to another attendee – to whom and about what I don't recall – when all of a sudden I felt this strong push against my chest and I instinctively closed my eyes, felt my body fly off the ground and I landed perfectly in this very comfortable chair directly behind me (although I didn't know it was behind me as I was flying through the air for that two or three seconds). I opened my eyes and saw the laughing face of Ken Wapnick standing over me. That's when I knew Ken really loved me. (Ladies, this practice of pushing is more a guy thing so you might not understand it as much as we of the male gender.) I honestly don't recall the next minute or so but here's a good guess: Ken reached down and pulled me up, gave me a hug and ruffled my hair. I know he didn't spend much time with me because he had another 200 plus people who he either knew personally or wanted to know who were all milling around during the break.

Another fond memory I have at one of Ken's teaching sessions in California occurred again during one of the breaks between sessions. Again, for those readers who never attended any of these sessions, please note that Ken always interspersed his teachings with a question and answer period wherein he answered questions from attendees. I invariably had something to say during these sessions – I am not a shy person. Apparently, through these public verbal exchanges between Ken and I, it was obvious that Ken and I were very good friends because during a break a number of people asked me about Ken and how we had become such good friends. This made me realize even more how fortunate I was to have Ken take such a keen interest in me.

I must say I felt so privileged when Ken took the time to read the draft of a book I wrote and offer helpful suggestions. The book was over 200 pages long. (This book was written under a pen name because it compared my 12-step program with the *Course* and an important tradition in 12-step programs is that we remain anonymous at the public level.)

Prior to this, I did appreciate how busy a man Ken must be what with his writing of books, his teaching sessions at the Foundation for *A Course in Miracles* (FACIM), his management responsibilities on behalf of the FACIM, his other pen pals with whom he corresponded, his articles in the FACIM monthly newsletter and his reviewing of *Course* books drafted by other *Course* students.

The only real time I got to spend with Ken one-on-one was the week after his teaching session in the spring of 2013. Although I had been trying to have a meal with Ken (or with Ken and his wife Gloria) over the prior year or so, this had not yet happened. However, on this trip to California I was staying an extra week and Ken and I had lunch together at a very nice Italian restaurant. The most memorable part of that one hour lunch for me was a very simple question I asked Ken which was "Do you still study *the Course*?" to which he replied simply "Yes, except when I'm writing a new book." This was important to me because for about 14 years at that time I had been studying *the Course* over and over and I didn't know of anyone else who did the same thing. (There's nothing written in *the Course* that even suggests this is a good idea.) So, like me, Ken had made the study of the *Course* a "way of life" although he started about 26 years before me.

At some point, and it may have been when we had lunch together, I remember Ken personally telling me that all I have to do is to accept Atonement for myself. This very simple suggestion, as I progress on the *Course*'s spiritual path, carries a very powerful message to me. So I'll pass this along to other *Course* students: "All you have to do is to accept Atonement for yourself." (Jesus spells this out in Workbook Lesson 139 – "I will accept Atonement for myself.")

I feel so very blessed and privileged to have had the benefit of knowing Ken as an exceptional friend and personal spiritual mentor. Ken's most important contribution to Jesus' *Course*, in my experience, has been the workshops he has given over the four decade period he taught the *Course*. I personally attended 4 of these, the last being in the spring of 2013. The wonderful thing is that most, if not all, of these workshops have been recorded by the Foundation for *A Course in Miracles* and are available to students of the *Course* now and for generations to come.

This Part II consists of two chapters:

Chapter 1: The Ken Wapnick letters – This includes 43 letters that Ken and I exchanged over our 2-year friendship; approximately half were from me to Ken and, naturally, the other half were from Ken to me.

Chapter 2: Duality as Metaphor in *A Course in Miracles* – This is the title of a multiple day workshop that Ken gave in 1993. It is available from the Foundation for *A Course in Miracles* and is approximately 11 hours in length. To date, I have listened to it 3 times and each time I have benefitted significantly because of its great depth; i.e., I strongly recommend it to other *Course* students. This chapter reflects some of the notes I took during the most recent time I listened to it, a few months ago.

Chapter 1: The Ken Wapnick letters

This chapter consists of 2 sections as follows:

Section A: Introduction

My "pen pal" letters back and forth to Ken represent nearly our entire relationship. Our mutual love for the *Course* was its foundation.

A few years before I met Ken in 2011, I had read Gary Renard's *The Disappearance of the Universe* book and met with Gary on 3 separate occasions – 2 weekend conferences where he was the sole teacher and one time when he had a 2 or 3 hour session during a convention with other well known spiritual teachers. In one of his books, his ascended master friends (Arten and Pursah) had told him he could count on 2 fingers the number of people who were really teaching the *Course* (ACIM). I figured, at the time, he (Gary) was one of them so I asked him who the other one was. I don't think he quite remembered the statement from his book but he answered without hesitation "It has to be Ken Wapnick." It was shortly after that when I started going to Ken's workshops in California. The first workshop I attended was in the spring of 2011.

I hope you enjoy these letters. I loved receiving Ken's letters to me and writing back to him. In Ken's letters, you can get a good idea of the type of person he was outside his role of teaching the *Course*. He was a fun loving, extremely happy guy. Although our friendship was wonderful, Ken was also my *Course* mentor during the two years we swapped letters. Clearly to me, there was no one better in the entire world. While there's some good *Course* material in some of the letters, for the most part I suggest you read these "for the fun of it!"

When I met Ken for the first time in the spring of 2011, I asked him before or between his teaching sessions if he thought my idea for a book which linked my 12-step spiritual program to ACIM was a good idea. Ken said "yes" and was a real motivating factor for me getting that book accomplished. This anonymous book is referenced a lot in the letters which follow. (Please note that this is now a published book but I use a pen name as author rather than my given name. In all the 12-step programs there is an anonymity tradition wherein we do not disclose our actual names at the public level.)

Here's a summary of ACIM which you can take literally: "When all is said and done, we'll all be living happily ever after forever and ever at Home in Heaven right where we all began." (Reasoning: Heaven is the only reality. All else is a dream from which we'll all wake up.)

Section B: The letters

Note that only very minor changes were made to the letters in order to protect my anonymity regarding the specific 12-step program of which I am a member.

There were 45 letters that Ken and I shared although I couldn't locate his last 2 letters to me. The other 43 letters that Ken and I shared are included in this section. For ease of reading, each letter begins on a new page.

<u>Ken Wapnick letter dated June 6, 2011</u>[1]

Dear Jimmy the Hat,

I know you won't get this until you get home[2], after completing your wonderful book, but I wanted to write anyway. Unfortunately, I don't do email[3] (did you know that I still balance my checkbook with an abacus?).

I hope your six weeks were good ones, and that while there you finally learned to do something with your hair[4]. It is always so messed up.

Hope to see you again, Jimmy.

Love,

Ken

[1]This is the first letter I received from Ken.

[2]I was on a 6-week trip with my wife and our little girl to Guyana, South America, which is my wife's native country.

[3]Shortly after attending my first session in Temecula – a 3-day session of Ken teaching a bunch of us about the *Course* – I sent Ken an email thanking him for all his help. That is why in this letter, he told me he doesn't do email. While I expect my email to Ken is out there in cyberspace somewhere, I have not been able to retrieve it for myself or I would have included it in this book.

[4]I learned from Gary Renard that when He saw Ken over the years, Ken would often ruffle his hair and, as I recall, tell him to lighten up. So when I introduced myself to Ken for the first time, I asked him if he wouldn't do the same for me which he gladly did. My take on this comment is that it is linked to that wonderful memory.

Dear Ken,

It's impossible to fully express in words how much your sessions in California and getting to know you a little personally have impacted my zeal for ACIM and also my zeal for getting my book completed.

Concerning the 3 days I spent with you in Temecula, your simple statement that "My ego says 'something happened' whereas God says 'nothing happened'" simplifies this whole dream world so much. So thank you for that and so much more, Ken.

When I got home 2 weeks ago and found your personal letter to me, I was so overjoyed that someone of your "importance" would take the time to send me a personal note. It was such a gift to me so thank you so much for that too.

We both know that if Jesus were to arrive at a gathering we were at he would tell us that we should not put him up on a pedestal. So I know you don't want me to put you up on a pedestal either but I sure do feel a kinship for you and for Gary Renard that goes way beyond the amount of time that we've been able to spend together. I love you guys.

In my personal life, I arrived back from Guyana 2 weeks ago and my wife, Tesha, and our little girl, Jimesha (who is 3-1/2), will return one week from today. As I have been reading the text of ACIM once again, I feel Jesus/the Holy Spirit telling me how important my Holy Relationship with Tesha is and will become in the future. Once she returns, we plan on spending some disciplined time reading the text of ACIM together again and probably follow that up with doing the lessons together again. Note that, following our engagement in early 2006, we spent about 14 months reading the text and doing the lessons together. Tesha, who is only 30, has since been much more involved in having babies and caring for our little Jimesha. We had one child who was stillborn in December of 2006 and another child who passed away after 2 months and 4 days in February of 2010. I don't know who Tesha was in any of her past lives but her forgiveness level probably still far exceeds my own. I have recently come to believe that she is my better half.

Anyway, regarding my book, I've got 104 type written pages done so far. My realistic plan is to have a draft of my 200 page book completed sometime in October. I must say I'm really enjoying putting it together and feel I'm benefitting a lot personally from the "work" (even if no one else reads it).

When I think about you and Gary, I know that you two guys have reduced the length of time that the dream world will have to continue by probably thousands of years as a result of your work with ACIM. Perhaps my book can also help to cut the time that we dreamers have to stay dreaming in this crazy world.

Now, I'm sure you'll never want to speak to me again because my book didn't get completed while I was in Guyana so I didn't meet your expectation (smile).

By the way, I fully understand that you don't do email and appreciate it so I'm sending this through regular mail. I do hope you read all of it though I tend to get long winded.

Do you really know how to use an abacus?

In addition to spending a lot of time on my book in Guyana, I had a wonderful 6 weeks there – What a deal!

My hair is still quite messy but when Tesha comes home next week, she'll give me a haircut and help me clean up my act.

By the way, Ken, my plan is to be out to visit you at one of your sessions again either later this year or the early part of next year. Meanwhile, please have fun and keep up the good work my happy friend.

Thank God for God, Who we effectively are.

Love,

Jimmy "the hat"

Ken Wapnick letter dated August 1, 2011

Dear Jimmy the Hat,

Thank you for your lovely letter and kind words. I guess when all is said and done you're probably not a bad guy, and who knows, maybe even a Son of God. And that would probably hold even if you didn't finish your book, which you had better do, otherwise you will have to deal with me. And remember, thee of the sexy hat, that I am from Brooklyn and my wife is Sicilian – you wouldn't stand a chance, Jimmy!

Thanks again for writing, and I look forward (I think) to your next visit. Happy writing! And give Tesha a hug for me, even though she probably thinks I'm a bit strange (which I am!).

Love,

Ken

P.S. As for that abacus, I'll never tell!

<u>Jimmy Laws letter dated August 28, 2011</u>

Dear Ken,

Thank you so much for your letter of August 1, 2011. Your influence on me continues to be powerful and I thank God for you so much.

My book progress is right on target – I'm completing two type written pages a day so that, at this rate, on September 13th I will have completed the 200 pages of my book draft. Following that, I will have to put together an introduction and review the draft to finish the final draft.

While at Disney World last week with my family, I dictated a chapter which I have tentatively titled "A Chat with Jesus." In that chat, Jesus instructed me to send you a copy of that chapter, which will tell you more about me and my understanding of the Course, no later than tomorrow (barring any worldly emergencies). It is therefore attached and I would greatly appreciate it if you would read those 16 pages and give me some feedback on it. I'm quite sure you will enjoy it – It is really an interview where Jesus is the interviewer and I am the interviewee. (Please note that, over the past month, I watched once again the interview that you and Gloria did with Corrine Edwards many years ago and really enjoyed it again. Two points – (1) I wanted to see if there was any mention of an "abacus" habit by you (smile), and (2) I thought Gloria was real cute when she used the word "thunk" (smile).

I've also sent you a copy of a September, 2011 magazine article. I was privileged to have this article I wrote included in this 12-step magazine. You can note that it tells how my 12-step program allowed me to get through the loss of our two babies in recent years. If you read the 3 pages of that article, you'll get a better understanding of my life without drugs or alcohol and the importance of my 12-step program to a guy like me.

Now, on to your own personal issues. Thank you for sharing that Gloria is Sicilian – I want you to know that I love Italians with their love for partying and so on. I can understand how being married to an Italian gal would keep you on the "straight and narrow." This got me to thinking – I'm not sure if the spelling is right but "Was Mrs. Bobbitt (sp?) Italian?"

Now, I'm sure I can help you on your abacus problem. Clearly, you have a tremendous fear of electronic devices. As you probably know, there are many 12-step programs in the world today. However, I'm quite certain there is none that covers the issue that you have where you're afraid to use electronic calculators and, therefore, rely on an abacus. You can therefore become the founder of "The Second AA Program in the World" and it will be referred to as "AA – Abacus Anonymous" – LOL! LOL!

I do think Tesha thinks you're strange - She already knows I am. I say this because, when I opened your August 1st letter, Tesha was right there with me so I read it out loud. When I read the sentence "I guess when all is said and done you're probably not a bad guy, and who knows, maybe even a Son of God", I laughed out loud. That was really funny to me and Tesha was just looking at me with a perplexed look so it appears you and I share the same strange sense of humor which is not shared by everyone else.

God bless you and Gloria, Ken.

Love,

Jimmy "the hat" Laws

Attachments: "A Chat with Jesus" and September, 2011 magazine article.

Dear Jimmy the Hat (and writer),

This will have to be short (you'll forgive me, right?) as I am out of town for a week. Thank you for sending the Jesus interview and magazine article – both real fine.

What else could I say? You want me to say something critical about Jesus? I may have grown up in the Brooklyn schoolyards, but I'm not *that* tough! Anyway, I enjoyed both of them, and they have whet my appetite for *more*! So quit stalling and finish the damn book!

And I'm afraid there is no hope for my abacus problem. You can still pray for me, though.

Thanks again, Jimmy.

Love,

Ken

P.S. And do tell Tesha that your strange (as in *very* strange) friend says hello.

Jimmy Laws letter dated September 20, 2011

Dear Ken,

Thank you very much for your letter of September 1, 2011. You asked me, jokingly I think, if I would forgive you because your letter was short. Trust me when I say I am thrilled (!) that perhaps the leading emissary of Jesus since Jesus' departure, namely Ken Wapnick, is having personal correspondence with me, Jimmy "the hat." So there was no concern on my part that your letter was not lengthy.

However, let's suppose that I did hold some grievance against you, just for arguments sake. Well, I know (although I can forget this from time to time) that I made you up from my mind and you're a part of my gigantic dream. By the way, I'm really glad that I made you up, Ken. You've already become a good friend. Since I made you up, if I hold a grievance against you, then clearly I'm holding a grievance against me. I am certainly the only problem I will ever have on planet earth.

You also used a profanity in your letter and I quote "So quit stalling and finish the damn book!" What came to mind immediately was the Corrine Edwards interview with you and Gloria. You may not recall the question, but Corrine asked you and Gloria if, as a student of A Course in Miracles, you were allowed to use profanity. Wisely, I thought, neither one of you answered that question. I certainly knew the answer was "sure." Now, with this September 1 letter of yours, I see that you agree with me. So, the damn draft of the damn book is attached. I hope you enjoy reading it.

I want to thank you for pushing me to get it done quicker than I anticipated. I worked hard to get this book out to you by tomorrow. You see I'm leaving in two days for a trip to Montana for a 12-step convention in Helena, Montana. Following the weekend convention, I'm taking an extra week for myself in that Montana "neck of the woods." Tesha and Jimesha will be here at home getting a break from this strange man.

I also want to thank you and your office staff for the *Concordance of A Course in Miracles*, which I purchased back in 2008. It really came in handy as a reference when I was working on parts of my book draft.

I think of our job as to help reduce "time" by helping others understand "truth" utilizing ACIM principles. Since it's so much fun, this I see as my special function for the remainder of this lifetime. This may be repetitious but

I'll point out that Jesus was clearly God's most important "physical" emissary 2,000 years ago and I see you as God's most important "physical" emissary in today's world. Therefore, I would certainly appreciate guidance from you as to how I might best help in this incredible movement.

Please note that I can write future articles and books using my real name and keep the name of my 12-step program out of it. (This current draft book, if it gets published, must remain anonymous because it includes the name of my specific 12-step program affiliation.)

Before I forget, Tesha loved your September 1 letter. She really enjoys strange people because she married one so I know she'll like you. For this reason, I'm sure Gloria will like me (if she likes you).

Here's 3 potential ideas I have for extending the principles of ACIM to the masses:

(1) Mosquitoes – I briefly reviewed your article in the September issue of THE LIGHTHOUSE newsletter called "THE LITTLE THINGS OF GOD: Forgiving All People and All Things." Because I've been working on the "damn" book, I'll be honest and say I didn't read and study the entire article. (I hope you'll be able to forgive me? ☺) Your article is consistent with ACIM which is quite esoteric whereas the truth or Heaven or Love is super simple. My primary question here is "Can we put together material which covers all the spiritual principles of ACIM in a simplified form?" For example, I could probably write an article, if so inspired, using ACIM principles which would discuss the question "How do I forgive mosquitoes?" This question, I would think, would catch people's attention and the article, I would expect would be fairly brief.

(2) This idea occurred to me as a result of an acronym I've been using, especially with our little girl Jimesha who will be 4 in November. If I ask her what frog means to her, she will spout out "Fully Relying On God." I've got an idea for a series of illustrated children's books where the main character is a frog named "FROG" who interacts with children and others and is full of wisdom from ACIM. We would say he is an enlightened frog.

(3) This third idea is a book entitled "A Course in Miracles for Dummies." My gut thinking on this is that it would contain 3 books like the full ACIM book but using simpler words and probably fewer pages and perhaps even less than 365 Lessons. This, of course, would be a pretty major undertaking.

Since all my thoughts, and yours too my friend, should be passed by Jesus (while ignoring our ego's insanity) I guess we'll find out if any of these ideas make sense. Also, it's quite possible that somewhere out there in the ACIM community, information like this is already being put together. I don't know because I have not been close at all to the ACIM community to date.

Please, once you've reviewed the attached book draft, offer suggestions as to what my next step should be. This would be very much appreciated, Ken. If you respond with "I think you should put this book up there 'where the sun don't shine' ", then I would understand that you really didn't like it. ☺ ☺

Based on my schedule, I would like to come out there to enjoy your teaching sessions on January 7-10 or February 11-14 or March 11-16. I can stay an extra week or more if this would give us time to have some individual get togethers and establish some future endeavors for me, if this appeals to you after you've read my book. (Perhaps I'll bring an abacus so you can teach me how to use it.☺)

Meanwhile, my family and I are having fun in the sun here in Florida and I hope you and Gloria are doing the same over there in California.

God bless you and Gloria, Ken.

Love,

Jimmy "the hat" Laws

/Attachment: Book Draft

Dear Jimmy the Hat,

As we usta say in Brooklyn:

MAZEL TOV[1]!!!!!!!!!!!!!!!!!

And I know you are such a forgiving guy, I know you will forgive me if it is a little while until I can read your damn *magnum opus*. Right? Unfortunately, this is a very busy time for me, and I have other manuscripts I have to read as well. But I look forward to this latest from the hat of Jimmy the Hat, and I shall happily read it as quickly as I can.

You won't receive this putrid excuse for a letter until after your very successful trip (I peaked!).

As for your next projects, I certainly like #s 1 and 2 (forgiving mosquitoes is a wonderful topic – I once did a workshop on forgiving gypsy moths – and I love the FROG idea).

#3, however, has been tried many times before and I am not so sure well serves the Course or your readers. But we can discuss it all when you come. Just so you know, my chapeau-laden friend, we would probably have to confine ourselves to one visit, as there are usually a lot of people for me to meet with. Canst thou find it, still once again, in thine heart of hearts to forgive me?

But first things, first – your book. And then we'll talk. Meanwhile, keep smiling at the world's silliness (after all, kiddies will be kiddies).

Oh, I loved your joke about having a "job" or "special function." That really made me laugh. Bet you thought I had forgotten about T-2-V.5:1[2]. Ah, you sneaky devil, you! So, did I pass the test?

Happy accepting! And while you're at it, do give Tesha one of my really strange hugs. And one for you, my strange friend!

Love,

Ken

[1]I had to look up 'Mazel Tov.' It's a Hebrew expression meaning 'Congatulations; good luck.'

[2]T-2-V.5:1 reads as follows: "*The sole responsibility of the miracle worker is to accept the Atonement for himself.*" The next sentence (T-2-V.5:2) adds significantly to the meaning of this: "This means you recognize that mind is the <u>only</u> creative level, and that its errors are healed by the Atonement." (I added the underscore emphasis to the word "only.") Although I didn't understand it at the time, now (5+ years later) it's much clearer that the "special function" which is defined in T-25.VI has *absolutely nothing* to do with any physical activity or job or action or words we say but, rather, *it has everything to do with how we think*. When my mind is one with Jesus and the ego therefore has no influence on me, I am achieving my "special function." In his last paragraph, where Ken tells me 'Happy accepting!', he's telling me to 'accept Atonement for yourself' which also tells me to be only guided by Jesus which in turn means I will be happy beyond anything the world has to offer.

<u>Jimmy Laws letter dated October 5, 2011</u>

Dear Miracle Ken,

Thank you very much for your letter of September 27, 2011.

Although I had heard the words MAZEL TOV before, I didn't know what they meant so I looked them up. Thank you. And although I knew what the word "damn" meant, I didn't know what the words "magnum opus" meant so I looked that up and thank you for describing my many "symbols of symbols" book as a great work.

Now I need to get this off my chest! I need to give you a piece of my mind! I will never be able to forgive you again if you ever ask me to forgive you again! That's silly, isn't it? 😊😊

Thank you for your comments on my 3 ideas and I've been thinking about ideas 1 and 2. Idea 3, "ACIM for Dummies", after you had told me it's been oft tried in the past and your suggestion that it ain't a good idea, I remembered that Arten and Pursah talked about any change to the Course being a bad idea. Thank God! I've therefore given up that idea.

When I made reference to a job or "special function", essentially spreading the "Good News" of ACIM as you've been doing for many decades now in my dream, I didn't mean it as a joke. 😊😊 What I was thinking about was the definition of "special function" that Jesus talks about in T-25-VI.4. It's possible I've misinterpreted this paragraph[1]. What do you think? So, did I pass the test?

I was just thinking today about the concept that Gary, Arten and Pursah discussed at some length of parallel "dream worlds."[2] Please let me know if the following makes sense to you. There's a real good chance that there's a parallel dream world out there where Jesus stepped back and let Mary Magdalene take the lead and Mary became the crucified Messiah rather than Jesus? Or there's a world where Mary and Jesus, together, got crucified and became joint Messiahs (like described in Chapter 11 of Revelations)? Personally, I really like the following world – Alcoholics Anonymous, in its current 12-step form, began right around the time Jesus was born. Following Jesus crucifixion, while on his way to hang himself with tremendous guilt and remorse, Judas runs into an AA member and ends up getting sober via AA rather than hanging himself. The 12-step spiritual formula becomes a major taproot towards "waking from that dream world" for the balance of that world. What do you think? (P.S. Tesha's comment on these ideas was – You're going to blow Ken's mind. Please let me know if this happens. ☺☺)

Oh yeah – You indicated that you knew I had a very successful trip to Montana. Yes I did – it was a wonderful trip! You say you "peaked." The best thing that comes to mind is that you have the ability of "mind transport" in the same fashion that Gary Renard was transported at least a couple of times by Arten and Pursah – one to Portland, Maine (as I recall) and another time to that Indian mound near St. Louis. Did you actually transport yourself to Montana and see me for a little while? You're silly enough and quite possibly spiritual enough to have done something like that. I actually believe that what I've suggested here is a good guess though I've never experienced anything like this whatsoever in this lifetime.

Here's one I really like and I think you'll enjoy – I sometimes tell people the following story of my birth: "I was actually born on a sheep ranch in Scotland! And to this very day, my mother has never told me who my D..a..a..a..a..d..d..y..y..y..y..y is." LOL! LOL! And we all laugh. I don't ever recall this joke backfiring. I then automatically point out that I was actually born in Brooklyn, like yourself. It appears there are a lot of strange people born in Brooklyn…LOL…LOL.

And "Happy Accepting" right back at you which today I think of as "Happy Forgiving."

My current plans are to fly into California about January 5th and stay 2 weeks – Tesha and Jimesha will hang back (partly 'cause Jimesha's in pre-school 3 mornings a week). I hope you'll be able to schedule me in for an individual session then – if not, I'll likely postpone it. I also hope you're social calendar isn't packed because I would really like to take you and Gloria, your much prettier half, out for dinner on an evening of your choice?

In any event, please give Gloria a big hug and a kiss for me. (That is, if kissing is okay in accordance with your Jewish traditions – LOL! LOL! I'm trying to be sillier in this letter. Have I gone overboard yet? If so, please forgive me.☺☺)

Friendship and Love,

Jimmy "the hat" Laws

[1]Today, I can answer my own question – Yes, I have misinterpreted paragraph T-25-VI.4. One of the simplest and very powerful statements in this Section VI is: "Forgiveness is the only function meaningful in time." [T-25-VI.5:3] This means to me that once I've attained 'complete forgiveness' in this world, I'll be fulfilling my 'special function' 100%. An important teaching I received from Ken is that we all have the same 'special function' – that my 'special function' was no different than his. To define 'special function' as 'complete forgiveness' is, of course, consistent with Ken's teaching.

[2]Regarding the idea of parallel "dream worlds", there is one reference in the *Course* to this type of idea as follows: "Atonement works all the time and in all dimensions of time." [T-1-I.25:2] Jesus clearly tells us there are different dimensions of time but he never expands on this. Using simple common sense, even if there are a near infinite number of parallel universes, I think I'm in this one and so do you or you wouldn't be reading this book so I think I'll just stay in this one for now.

Ken Wapnick letter dated October 10, 2011

Dear Jimmy the Hat, the Silly One,

Your letters are getting funnier and funnier, you know that? I really guffawed over that stuff about Jesus and Mary, as if they were their real names, real people and the like. What an imagination thou hast? Tesha was certainly right, except not that you blew my mind, but my sides – from laughing so hard. You're good. You almost had me going there with thinking that there was actually a past[1]. You're not good, funny man with the funny hat, you're *very* good!

As for what I did in Montana, you almost got me again – not only believing in a world of time, but one of space. How could a person transport anywhere when there ain't no anywhere to transport to[1]? Again, you are real, real good.

Getting together during the first half of January sounds like a plan, Jimmy, assuming, that is, that there will be a world to hang out in in 2012. But perhaps you're doing your funny time and space thing again.

Toodles, funny man.

Love,

Ken

[1] As Jesus puts it so succinctly in Workbook Lesson 132: "There is no world! This is the central thought the course attempts to teach." [W-132.6:2-3]

Dear Miracle Ken,

Thank you and Jesus/Holy Spirit very much for your letter of October 10, 2011. It has helped me tremendously!

This letter is broken up into a number of different subjects as follows.

My Past History with You in My Dream

Around Easter time in the year 2008, I attended Gary Renard's weekend session out near Joshua Tree National Park and had a wonderful time. Following that, I spent another week or so in your neck of the woods and stopped at the Foundation for ACIM there in Temecula for the primary purpose of meeting you. (I was not known as Jimmy "the hat" in those days.) As I recall, I had to wait a while for you to show up and then you were able to give me about 2 or 3 minutes of your time in the bookstore. During that time, you signed my ACIM book, not that anyone can read your writing ... ☺. I asked you one question which you might recall: "Are you enlightened yet?" and your response, as I recall, was: "I don't know." I remember you as being this very happy and very busy man and you told me you really couldn't give me any time because of other commitments ..... and it was all good. Do you happen to recall that little incident?

Again, Thank You for Your Letter of October 10, 2011

I truly laughed out loud at your brief but powerful letter. I believe Tesha was there when I first read it out loud (for both of us) and she smiled too.

Thanks for not using too many big words and sticking to the English language ... LOL! ☺

I do understand your 1st paragraph which is "If the dream is a dream, then the dream is a dream and it ain't real." Another way to put this I think is "If there's only ONENESS, then there ain't no two of us and you, Miracle Ken, are me, Jimmy the hat, and we are "Jesus the first" and we are part of the Holy Spirit and We are part of God (our Source) .... And there is only ONENESS.

When I saw Gary Renard in the spring of this year up in Massachusetts, I think he said "We are God". For what it's worth, the words I use to describe this ONENESS to others goes like: "I am effectively God, the only difference being is God created me and I did not create God but in Heaven we don't even think about this difference. And you (whoever I'm talking to), my friend, are the same and we are just part of ONENESS."

I think I just figured it out. When you wrote that you knew I had a good time in Montana because you "peaked", it was a pun referring to all the mountain "peaks" there. Am I right? I had misread it as you had "peeked" at my life via some strange psychic ability – admittedly, you are strange, but perhaps not that strange ☺.

Shortly after I received your October 10th letter, Tesha and I were having a reading/study session with ACIM. At the beginning of that session, Tesha helped me realize I was getting too caught up in Gary Renard's journey. I should stick to ACIM and my own experiences. Your letter told me the same thing as I understand your letter. As a matter of fact, your letter tells me, as Jesus does in his ACIM book, that there are no "levels" but only the ONENESS of Heaven and everything else is but an illusion.

I'm sure you'll appreciate that, although we are currently asleep in Heaven dreaming our lives here, I have a lot of earthly plans coming up and I'd like to talk to you about them as regards A Course in Miracles and some of my own personal "issues." So, if you don't mind, for now I'll just use Jesus to mean my true inner Voice (Voice of God, Voice of the Holy Spirit or the Voice of Jesus). Don't laugh please. I'm trying to be a little serious here ☺.

In my 12-step program, we have a slogan which says: "You have to give it away to keep it." As I understand ACIM, Jesus often includes the same thought.

My Planned Trip to California in January, 2012

My plan is to fly into Southern California on Wednesday, January 4th, and return to Florida on January 11th. Within my dream, I need to be back here in Florida for a 12-step business convention beginning Friday, January 13th.

During my time in California, I plan to attend your 3-day session on "The Trojan Horse of Specialness" beginning Sunday, January 8th. Interestingly, about a week ago, I watched for I think the second time the movie "Troy" before I noticed the title of your sessions I'll be attending. I gather from the movie that the Trojan Horse was fictional from the "Iliad" book? So in worldly terms, the Trojan Horse was fiction. What you and I know is that the whole world is fiction – Thank you Jesus for pointing this out to us (and to Helen and Bill for all their hard work in getting ACIM published for us, and to you, Ken, for your lifelong commitment to this incredible book and its forward movement).

Foundation for ACIM Bookstore Here in Southwest Florida

Have you ever considered starting another ACIM bookstore in other parts of the U.S., for example here in Southwest Florida? I wouldn't mind getting involved in that at some level if you thought it was a good idea. You could have all of the same literature and tapes that you have in your bookstore there in Temecula. Ultimately, you could of course have some teaching/learning sessions like you have out there in California.

It would be a good way to expand ACIM to another part of the world.

Jimmy the Hat's Personal Habits

I really enjoy smoking cigarettes and drinking coffee. I've especially been criticized for smoking cigarettes but it does not appear to be affecting my physical health at any significant level.

I recently finished reading through the preface and the 3 books of ACIM again. For the first time, I read through the Workbook for Students as a textbook (rather than doing the daily lessons) and it was an exceptionally good experience for me. I started the preface on June 4, 2011 and finished the Teacher's Manual on October 19, 2011 (which was my 62nd birthday in this life's episode of my dream).

In the past, please note that I've read the URTEXT a number of times, your *Absence of Felicity* book and, for a while, I studied the Lessons with the help of your "Study Books" which help clarify the Lessons. Where were your "silly jokes" when I needed them? LOL! LOL! ☺ ☺ Your published works don't give a clue what a fun guy you truly are. Of course, the same can be said of Jesus' ACIM books.

My Ego Problem

My true inner voice (i.e., Jesus) seems to be telling me over the past few days that the primary problem I've had is when my ego tells me that I am the Teacher (rather than the Voice for God) and I attempt to control the lives of other people. While this happens on a much lower scale than it used to, it's still a problem for me sometimes. So please, Kenny, don't let me push you around too much – OK, brother? LOL … ☺ I'm still a "Work in Progress."

By contrast, you're probably listening to your ego a whole lot less than I've been listening to my ego.

Sometimes I "don't act appropriately" in Tesha's opinion and it annoys her. She usually lets me know after the fact when we're alone so it's easy for me to tell her: "Well, Tesha, it's a spiritual axiom that anytime you're disturbed, no matter what the cause, there's something wrong with you." Then I laugh out loud – however, I do listen to her and it affects my conduct in future social situations so I believe I'm becoming a "More Appropriate Person." That's funny isn't it? Perhaps the title of my next adult book will be "How to Become a More Appropriate Person" by Jimmy "the Hat" Laws assisted by his lovely bride from South America, Tesha "Besha" Laws. LOL! LOL! ☺

In fact, of course, Tesha is a real treasure to me and a great teacher for me. So is our little Jimesha who will be 4 on November 5th – Jimesha and I cooked a meat loaf dinner last night for Tesha and a friend of ours from St. Martin who is staying with us for a while; a lovely young single gal named Shonette. Jimesha and I had a blast cooking this meat loaf dinner.

<u>My Book Draft</u>

How are you doing on this? Have you finished reading it? Have you started? Have you thrown it in the trash?

I was thinking I should probably criticize you for the sentence structure and language in your last letter. In the second paragraph you included the following phrase: "... when there ain't no anywhere to transport to?" Now, any good English teacher would have your head handed to you for writing that sort of thing. (Back in Brooklyn, you must have been told that "ain't" ain't a word.) How could you? LOL! ☺☺

But check this out – Last Thursday, I was reading the chapter in my book on the spiritual statements contained in my 12-step literature because I had to tell my story at a 12-step meeting that night and I wanted to refresh my memory. As I read that chapter, I noticed that at one point, instead of writing the word "outweigh", I wrote "out way." LOL! [A dyslexic hippy might say "Way out, man!" if he read this as it's currently written. In any event, I know you chose your words for both their honesty and their silliness – God bless you, my very good man.

While I hope to receive some valuable input from you concerning my draft book, I do think that Jesus wants me to read through it again and make some changes to it (and perhaps not just typos such as I just described). But, at this point, I'm waiting for input from you, perhaps when we get together in January.

Here's an idea. Perhaps these letters can be put into a book because others can benefit from them too. There's a lot of laughter in our letters which is generally "good" medicine. How's this for a title: "Miraculous Correspondence Between Dr. Miracle Ken Wapnick and Jimmy Laws." What do you think, Miracle Ken?

By the way, as I've reflected on the thoughts I've expressed in my book, there is an obvious lie in the book. If it doesn't jump out at you after you've read the book, I'll tell you what it is – Okay? It's a big one. You may have noticed some others which I'm not aware of.

The FROG Book

You will recall I expect, because you thought it was a good idea, the possible project for me of writing a children's book based on FROG, a frog who Fully Relies On God. In the terminology used in Gary's books, he would be considered an "ascended master" frog. He befriends a little girl named Jimesha and Jimesha learns a lot about the truth or the ONENESS from him based on Jesus' teachings from ACIM.

In order to prepare myself for this book, I decided to work on my ability to sketch characters and cartoons which I've never done before. However, about a year ago I picked up an introductory instructional sketching book at Disney World and used it to develop this artistic talent in me. What fun it's been!

I've attached to this letter copies (for your amusement and applause for me – Is this my ego?) of the cartoons I've drawn, the last one being the current version of FROG, himself. Please enjoy.

My plan is to complete a draft of the first "FROG book" by Christmas and have it as a Christmas present for my little girl, Jimesha. If you don't ask me to do anything on my book before then, it's a cinch that I'll get this FROG book done by then. It sure will be fun! So, what do you think about this, Ken? Are you going to give me any other homework before Christmas? Even if you do, there's a lot of time for everything that needs to be done on any given day – All I have to do is remember the spiritual axiom: "I need do nothing." So I can do absolutely nothing during a 24-hour day and I've done everything that needs to be done.

Silly Jokes

I was hoping that you'd at least comment on my "sheep" joke in my last letter. I can tell you that many many people have laughed at that joke. Although the majority of these people are people in my 12-step fellowship, there have still been many others who have got a good chuckle out of it. Perhaps most important, I always get a good chuckle when I tell it. So what was your reaction?

Here's one that is absolutely clean. You can tell it to a 5-year old and they'll likely laugh at it. And you have my permission to use this one just as you can feel free to use my "sheep" joke. LOL! ☺ ☺ Here it is: "In New York City, there's a big park, called Central Park, and it is a very dangerous place to walk in after dark. Well, one night, there were 2 peanuts walking in Central Park because they didn't heed the warnings of others telling them what a bad idea it was to walk there at night. As a result, one of them got assaulted! LOL! LOL! Ha! Ha! Ha!" [Get it, Ken? Assaulted is like "a salted" as in "salted peanuts". If you require further explanation, I'll tell you when I see you in January. LOL! LOL! ☺ ☺]

Our Travel Plans for Next Spring/Summer

Our plans are to take a 3-month road trip from mid-April (2012) until mid-July. During that time, we expect to be in your neck of the woods for a little while and hopefully you'll get a chance to meet these 2 wonderful gals in my life, Tesha and Jimesha, and they will, of course, get a chance to meet you (I hope).

■■■

I sure hope we'll be able to get together one-on-one in January (even though there's no such thing as "2" in Truth) for a session. Please let me know.

Also, it truly would be my pleasure to take you and Gloria out for a meal at a local restaurant. Do you think this might be possible?

Thank you, Ken, for your incredible help in my understanding of A Course in Miracles and the "Oneness of Truth that Sets Us Free."

I sure hope you've been able to get some laughs out of this letter. If not, I'll certainly try and do better next time.

I love you brother,

Jimmy "the hat" Laws

P.S. Please improve your handwriting …. LOL! LOL! ☺ ☺
/Attachments – Cartoons from "New Up and Coming" Cartoon Artist

Ken Wapnick letter dated November 1, 2011

Dear Jimmy the Hat, my most appropriately inappropriate friend,

Thank you for yet another wonderful letter, and thank you for forgiving me for yet another brief, boring one.

Sure, when you're here we can get together. I don't know about a meal, since Gloria and I usually get all booked up at these things. But you can never tell. Sorry to say I have not begun your *magnum opus* (which means big book in this context), but will certainly do so before our meeting, if not before. Thank you for being so patient with me. If I didn't hang out at the bars so much I'd probably get a lot more done![1]

Anyway, when you are here we can talk about all the wild stuff in your wild letter. And I can't wait to meet the wonderful ladies in your life next summer. I hope they like me and haven't believed all the awful things you told them about me.

As for your sheep joke, I thought you were serious (your having written a very serious letter, being an oh-so-serious guy), and since seriousness scares the hell out of me, I am afraid that it went out of my mind the minute it threatened to disturb my peace. But my memory is that it was quite a story, just like that very sad story about the two assaulted peanuts. *C'est dommage!*

Meanwhile, Happy FROG-GING!

Give big hugs to Tesha and dear little Jimesha, and a kick in the ass for you (That's for those poor peanuts).

Love,

Ken

[1]This was an inside joke. Ken, of course, was not in the habit of hanging out in bars but he knew this was a great habit of mine until I grabbed hold of my 12-step program in 1997.

<u>Jimmy Laws letter dated November 22, 2011</u>

Dear Miracle Ken, my silliest serious friend,

I sure hope you and Gloria had a wonderful Thanksgiving. Also, as we enter this Holiday Season, I certainly wish you both the happiest Holiday weeks you've ever had to date.

Thank you very much for your letter of November 1, 2011. Your letters are not boring at all from my end. While they are fairly brief, I fully understand as you're a busy guy.

Wow! Life is really a lot of fun for me today. I mean my dream life, naturally, and I'm really glad that I "made you up" in my dream. You're a great character, you silly man, you. ☺ You've probably seen the movie, *Funny Girl*, with Barbara Streisand? Anyway, it's a classic and a lot of fun. I think you and I could do a movie together called *Funny Men*.

I actually have a few serious questions and comments concerning ACIM.

<u>Technical Questions/Comments Regarding ACIM</u>

I have some confusion in my mind in interpreting that portion of the Text starting with paragraph 4 of Chapter 2.IV (Healing as Release from Fear) and extending through paragraph 2 of Chapter 2.V (The Function of the Miracle Worker).

The first sentence in paragraph 4 of Section IV reads "All material means that you accept as remedies for bodily ills are restatements of magic principles."

Sentence 6 of paragraph 2 of Chapter 2.V. reads "As long as your sense of vulnerability persists, you should not attempt to perform miracles."

My experience this year includes the following: (1) I had a cold which didn't want to quit though it didn't slow me down too much. Finally, I went to my doctor and he quickly determined that it was a sinus infection and he gave me antibiotics which knocked out the sinus infection. (2) Currently, I have some "athlete's foot" between 2 of my toes and I apply the appropriate over-the-counter meds which I'm certain will do the job because I get this about every 2 years. (3) Here in Florida, we have quite a bit of a mosquito problem. I'm in the habit of spraying mosquito spray on me before I go out at night and this works – mosquitoes stay away from me.

As I see it, in all 3 of these situations, I've used "material means" as remedies for bodily ills. Is the following statement consistent with what Jesus is saying in the Course – When I attain the "Jesus level of spirituality", I won't need any internal medicines or external ointments and sprays to resolve any such annoyances?

This next question has to do with the Voice or Voices of Jesus and the Holy Spirit. I like to think of Them as the same Voice. In my most recent reading of the Text, I came across this distinction between the Holy Spirit and Jesus: The Holy Spirit reminds me of God's fairness and Jesus teaches me to share it with others. (Though I made a note of this, I didn't write down the chapter, section, paragraph and sentence or sentences. Will you ever be able to forgive me? ☺) In your experience, are there 2 Voices or 1 Voice?

It seems to me that one of the most important things that we, as students of ACIM, can tell others about this incredible book is "Hey people – This is a self-study course!" What do you think? As I recall, Arten and Pursah made a strong point of this but I don't recall seeing it said anywhere else.

Also, as I recall, Arten and Pursah said that ACIM is the only teaching (ever!) that tells us that my ego and everybody's ego is itself an illusion. Is this accurate as far as you know?

Sentence 1 of paragraph 2 of Chapter 4.VI. reads "In learning to escape from illusions, your debt to your brother is something you must never forget." I must tell you that this debt that I owe to my brother and, in particular, to sick and suffering addicts and alcoholics like I was, is a wonderful part of my life today. In this regard, the 12-step meetings are such a tremendous training ground for meeting the sickest of our brothers and sisters. When first walking through the doors of our 12-step programs, we are physically, mentally and, of course, spiritually really messed up and our 12-step programs go a real long way towards straightening us out. What a deal!

This ends my serious stuff. Now for what I consider a good blonde joke:

A Good Blonde Joke

Three ladies, two brunettes and a blonde, walk into a busy bar so the bartender is very busy and impatient.

First brunette: "Hey bartender, give me a BW."

Bartender: "BW? What's a BW?"

First brunette: "A Budweiser, duh!"

Second brunette: "And give me a BL."

Bartender: "Jesus Christ! What's a BL?"

Second brunette: "A Bud Light, duh!"

Blonde (in a cute squeaky blonde voice): "And I'd like a 15 please."

Bartender: "For God's sake, what's a 15?"

Blonde: "A 7 and 7, duh!" LOL! LOL!

End Notes to my Favorite Pen Pal, Miracle Ken

Well, I've got my plane tickets so I'll be flying in on January 4th and returning home on January 11th and I've signed up for your January 8th, 9th and 10th educational sessions. I am really looking forward to it, too.

Please let me know, if you can, when we can have our one-on-one session during that time. Also, I would be very grateful if I could treat you or you and Gloria to a meal at a restaurant of your choice during the time that I'm there. If your time won't permit it, I will fully understand.

As you indicated in your last letter, you are really looking forward to meeting Tesha and Jimesha in the first half of next year when all 3 of us will be in your neck of the woods as a family. Attached is a picture of these 2 wonderful gals in my life.

I know this letter has been overly serious and I hope you can find some humor in that. I also hope you stay in my dream for many moons to come my brother.

With much love,

Jimmy "the hat" Laws

/Attachment – Picture of the 2 best gals in my dream life, Tesha and Jimesha.

P.S. Congratulations to The Foundation for Inner Peace for the release of the Chinese publication of ACIM and the ability to reach more than 1 billion people with it! Wow! Great news! You folks there at The Foundation are doing a wonderful great job in this physical world.

Ken Wapnick letter dated November 28, 2011

Dear Jimmy the Hat,

Your letters get longer and mine get briefer. I think I get so bogged down in the seriousness of it all (nothing more frightening than one who has been infected by the *seriousies*) that I am rendered speechless.

So I shall content myself (and then run like hell from those infernal, virulent creatures) with saying that you are making a big deal (those damn *seriousies* again!) about this magic stuff. When you are at that *Jesus level of spirituality* (whatever the hell that is), if your body is sick you take an aspirin, or something, and pay it no mind. Focus on your hat, my friend, *that is where the true action is.* Everything else is a defense against *that* hat. With it on, and properly placed on thy handsome head, you don't perform miracles (what could be sillier?), you *are* the miracle.

Yes, Jesus and the Holy Spirit are one Voice. Remember, They can't count past *one*. More than one (as in *two* Voices) make them very confused (like your letters are to me).

See you in January, sometime. I can't tell you when, though. Sorry. Besides, since the world will end in 2012, it probably doesn't much matter anyway.

Love,

Ken

P.S. What is this about one billion Chinese? There is only *one*. But you knew that. You were only testing me, you sneaky hat-laden person, you!

Jimmy Laws letter dated December 26, 2011

Dear Miracle Ken, my silliest serious friend,

First, let me thank you very much for your last letter. It really got me to thinking. It's not clear to me whether you were (a) Asking me for help because you're getting overly serious, or (b) Telling me I need help because I'm getting too serious? [It doesn't matter, of course, because you are me since God only has one Son which, I'm sure, you know already.]

I'm going to go with (a) just for the fun of it – you're asking me for help, okay? It's real simple, Ken. There is only Oneness or God or Heaven or Love or Truth or whatever other term you might want to give it. There is nothing else. The feeling is eternal bliss, never changing but forever expanding.

You are "living happily ever after" which you will fully appreciate when you wake up from your silly dream. End of story. (But I think you already know this and you were testing me. Right?)

I understand the magic stuff now, thanks to you. If, say, little Jimesha cuts her finger, I should put a band aid on it rather than just trying to pray the bleeding away, right? ☺

If you've read my draft book, you now know that the "Jesus level of spirituality" means attaining the "real world", being enlightened, being in the Holy Instant virtually all the time or one of the other myriad of terms used in ACIM.

Of course, you're right – There can't be one billion Chinese when there's only Oneness – You passed the test. And I really like the new test you gave me – You said the world will end in 2012. Now, Ken, how can something that doesn't even exist end? Duh! I passed, right?

I'm really looking forward to seeing you real soon, my good friend.

Love ya,

Jimmy "the hat" Laws

<u>Ken Wapnick letter dated December 29, 2011</u>

Dear Jimmy the Hat,

Yep, you got it. You is too damn serious! Especially about this oneness stuff. But at least you own stock in band-aids. They are very good, I am told, for cuts.

See you soon, my oh-so-serious friend with the wonderfully silly (and lovely) family.

Love,

Ken

Jimmy Laws letter dated January 19, 2012

Dear Miracle Ken,

I'm really glad you enjoy your work because I really enjoy your lesson sessions in Temecula and the happy banter between we two as well as your banter with all your other friends.

I also want to thank you immensely for reading my 2 draft books and your remarks concerning them. Please note that my current thinking is to complete the FROG book first but adding the following simple children's song to the spiritual teachings contained therein: "Row, row, row ya boat, gently down the stream. Merrily, merrily, merrily, merrily, life is but a dream." Of course, knowing we're only dreaming what we used to think of as life is a very important part of Jesus' ACIM. If you have any questions on this, please call me – LOL! LOL!

Hey, I figured out why my ego has made so many mosquitoes. At times in my spiritual awakening over the past 13 years, while studying or contemplating "deep" spiritual lessons, my mind and body have been totally annoyed by buzzing and biting mosquitoes. They have destroyed any possibility of staying at peace. Recently, I've learned that if I put mosquito spray on "before" I'm in a mosquito area, this problem is solved. Thank God for mosquito spray!

By the way, I'm no longer spending time with Tesha on studying ACIM. Rather, we're spending a lot of time together studying her GED material – I'm the tutor and she's the student and we're having fun doing it. Once she gets her GED, she might very well go to college. The thinking on this for me is that ACIM is definitely a self-study course and, once her English skills are enhanced, she will be in a better position to follow the journey of ACIM if that is her "destiny".

Are you and Gloria enjoying Pooh Bear (He's a wonderful listener I've found ☺) or have you handed him over to your grandson?[1]

Love ya,

Jimmy "the hat" Laws

[1]When I met with Ken in Temecula shortly before I wrote this letter, I gave him a Pooh Bear stuffed animal.

Dear Jimmy the Hat,

Yeah, it was pretty cool having you here for me to beat you up. We must do it again sometime.

Glad to hear that you have made your peace at last with the poor, beleaguered, much-maligned mosquito. The Sonship applauds thee, as do I. Some of my best friends are mosquitoes, so we all sing to thy holy self, atop which sits thy holy hat:

BRAVO!!!!!!!!!!!!!!!!!!!!!!

All of the rest of the stuff pales into insignificance when juxtaposed with this holy and well-deserved BRAVO!

And that's great about your finally releasing poor Tesha from the bonds of *A Course in Miracles*. Good for you, Jimmy, and even gooder for her! Besides, GED is much, much holier than ACIM. Just add up the numerical equivalent of the letters, divide by the number of letters, take the square root of that number, add up the digits of the square root, divide by the sum by the number of digits. And Voila! You will certainly understand my comment then.

Cheers, my oh-so-serious friend.

Love,

Ken

P.S. Nah, the Pooh Bear is for us'n!

<u>Jimmy Laws letter dated February 2, 2012</u>

Dear Miracle Ken,

I must tell you, my good friend and great teacher of ACIM, that you have really helped me take a giant leap towards "the real world" and "vision" when you told we students last month that the "Son of God is all living <u>and all non-living</u> things". It's hard to explain so let me just say thank you so very much.

Now, you will see what a good student I am and it is clear that GED is holier than ACIM if we're on the same wave length – in Truth, of course, we are because there's only one of us. Please note that the last part of your math instructions reads "divide by the sum by the number of digits" which I interpreted as a typo and assumed it should have read "divide the sum by the number of digits." Anyway, when I did the math, the result for GED was 3.6000 and the result for ACIM was 4.3333. Now, you and I know that there is only One (or Oneness) and, since the result for GED is closer to 1.0000 than the result for ACIM (3.6000 vs. 4.3333), it is certainly clear that GED is holier than ACIM. Did I pass this, your latest, test?

Hey, wonderful news for you and we – Both Tesha and I will be at your June 10, 11 and 12 lessons so you'll get a chance to meet this wonderful gal who's been putting up with me for nearly 6 years of marriage – Talk about miracles! LOL! We'll be there in your neck of the woods with our wonderful little girl, Jimesha the Sweetheart and giver of the gift of Pooh Bear, for 2 to 3 weeks I reckon; hopefully, we can get together with you and Gloria outside the classroom while we're there.

Love ya,

Jimmy "the hat" Laws

Copy – Tesha Laws

Ken Wapnick letter dated February 7, 2012

Dear Jimmy the Hat,

Glad I was finally of some help to thee. And I hope you realize that the inspiration for my comment was *your sacred hat.* Heaven forfend anyone leave its sacredicity (I channeled that word) out of the Sonship.

As for your math, I am afraid you flunked the test, my friend. I *did* mean to divide by the *sum* of the digits. So, back to the arithmetic drawing board with thee.

So sorry about June, but I have to attend a funeral during that weekend and so can't be there. Very tragic for the family! But perhaps another time will work out.

Love,

Ken

Jimmy Laws letter dated April 23, 2012

Dear Miracle Ken,

I certainly hope Gloria is doing better and that Pooh Bear is giving her some comfort. Personally, I often find that stuffed animals are good people to talk to. Please tell her I said hi and it would be great if our families can get together when we visit there in June – we fly in to John Wayne Airport on June 6th and fly home to Florida on June 27th.

Would it be possible for you and me to start having phone conversations periodically? While these letters are fun, they're quite time consuming, especially for me. I would very much appreciate it if the answer was 'yes.'

For the fun of it concerning our correspondence on your statement that "GED is much, much holier than ACIM" – You will recall perhaps that in your last letter (February 7th), you corrected the typographical error contained in your January 23rd letter so that for both GED and ACIM, we (1) Add up the numerical equivalent of the letters, (2) Divide by the number of letters (3 and 4, respectively), (3) Take the square root of the result, (4) Add up the digits of the square root, and (5) Divide by the sum of the digits. Clearly, all I need do is consider steps (4) and (5). In step (4), I've added up some digits and, in step (5), I've established the sum of those same digits and since "added up" means the same thing as "the sum", step (4) must equal step (5). Now, having the brilliant mathematical mind that I do (smile - ☺), I know that when the numerator and denominator in a division problem are identical, the resulting answer must be 1 (which, as you've stated in your classes is Jesus' spiritual math answer to everything. I think you said 2X2 equals ONE to Jesus which I understand because of the Truth of One Mind, One Love, etc. I'm convinced that in Heaven, my math skills are useless.) Now, Ken, if the result for both GED and ACIM is 1, how can GED be much, much holier than ACIM? You were just pulling our legs, right? Tesha and I are anxiously awaiting your answer to this important question – LOL!

I have a feeling you're trying to avoid me? In your last letter, you wrote "So sorry about June, but I have to attend a funeral during that weekend and so can't be there. Very tragic for the family! But perhaps another time will work out." I think you're pulling my leg here? But even if it were true, can't we just switch over to another dimension of time wherein you don't have to attend this future funeral? Good idea, eh?

I've been continuing my pure ACIM studies at a very good level and continue very active in my 12-step program. I've also been spending good time with Tesha and Jimesha. Tesha turned 31 on March 31st so we had a birthday party at our house – 65 people turned up and it was great fun!

During your January classes, someone suggested I read David Hoffmeister's book, *Awakening through A Course in Miracles,* which I did and really benefited from it.

Regarding my book, I modified my chapter on Gary Renard to exclude anything on reincarnation. You suggested I do this because, as Jesus talks about in his ACIM book, it's a controversial topic and people can awaken from their dream whether or not they believe in it. I've just decided (as I'm writing this letter to you) to take my belief in reincarnation out of the other chapter where it's mentioned – the chapter where Jesus interviews me.

I also read through my book and tweeked it here and there to make it more readable.

Finally, at your suggestion, I'll be adding a sub-section in the book on overcoming the ego's insane arguments. It seems that for most of us, and perhaps for all of us, the last hurdle to overcome is the thought that we have to overcome our "Individuality" which, of course, is true. About 1-1/2 years ago, after many years of studying ACIM, the question occurred to me: "Would I rather be an individual or would I rather be God?" I decided I'd rather be God .... Duh! LOL! I know I'm not God (the Source) but since He's given me, you, and all of us all that He has, we are all effectively God. Anyway, it's this type of thinking I'm planning to add as a section in my book. Any helpful hints here or other ideas?

Would you like to see the revisions to my book? When it's ready to go to print, will you publicly endorse it?

This paragraph and the next two touch on a few specifics from *ACIM*. (Note: Call me "anal" if you like but I virtually always answer Jesus' questions from his *ACIM* book, even his rhetorical ones – I write my answers in the margin of the book.) When Jesus asks "What can be more certain than a Son of God?" [T-20.IV.8.12], my answer was "God Himself...but We are one with Him." My Inner Voice (Jesus/Holy Spirit) said "Good answer – share this with Ken." So, in this letter, I've accomplished that instruction.

"The present is before time was, and will be when time is no more." [T-13.VI.7.5] After years of studying the Course, I'm finally grasping this concept – David's book really helped me here. The Holy Instant, when properly practiced, has nothing to do with time as I now understand it. On a similar note, I've been staying in touch with the fact that my worldly life is my dream during a higher percentage of the time. In the Teacher's Manual, Jesus says, as I recall, that the Teacher of God's primary function is to remain aware that he/she's dreaming.

"No one can stand before this obstacle alone (i.e., the 'fear of God' obstacle), for he could not have reached this far unless his brother walked beside him." [T-19.IVD.9.2] I also make notes in other places when reading *ACIM*, not just when Jesus asks questions. While clearly, I've had many people help me on my journey, please smile because I made a note in my *ACIM* book when I read this sentence to indicate "Jesus and Ken Wapnick" as two of my brothers who have walked beside me. You have had a major impact on me, Ken, and for this I am eternally grateful.

Tesha is looking forward to attending your June classes as well as me. You'll love her. Having read all our correspondence, I think she thinks you might be even crazier than me – LOL!

Love ya,

Jimmy "the hat" Laws

Copy – Tesha Laws

Ken Wapnick letter dated April 26, 2012

Dear Jimmy the Hat,

So you're still coming in June, even though I have this terribly tragic funeral. Ah the pain of the family! Perhaps you can send flowers.

Sure we can speak on the phone, ol' buddy. Just so you know that unfortunately I do not have a lot of time. But since time is illusory, as you have taught me, I'm sure we will manage just fine. Just be sure to wear your hat.

As for GED and ACIM, I am afraid that you have confused *fasnarvitz* with *tzimmisses*, which is why you think 4 is 5, and 5 is 4. But I still love you.

I don't have to see the revisions unless you would like me to. And I am very sorry, but for over thirty years I have had the policy of never publicly endorsing anyone or anyone's work. Canst thee find it in thine heart of hearts to forgive me?

Love,

Ken

P.S. Tell Tesha it is not that I might be crazier than you. I AM CRAZIER THAN YOU! Just look at whom I hang around with!

<u>Jimmy Laws letter dated May 17, 2012</u>

Dear Miracle Ken,

I know our dreams were over a long time ago so it's possible you know you'll be at a funeral come June 10,11 and 12th during your next scheduled classes in Temecula. I hope not, though, because I get a lot of good stuff at your teachings and I'm sure Tesha will too. Perhaps, you've just been pulling our legs on the funeral bit?

We have some important news which actually segways into my wonderful book. About 2 weeks ago I asked Tesha to ask Jesus if she should try and get pregnant this month and she said that he said 'yes' so it's possible Tesha is pregnant now – we'll know in about 2 weeks. I estimate our cost to have our new baby will be in the neighborhood of $30,000 and it would be good if I could get some income from the book to pay for some or all of this.

I have included my most recent draft of the book. One change I made was to use a more traditional ACIM reference format than what I had in my 1st draft. The reference system is described on the second page of the book's <u>Introduction.</u> I've also changed Appendix II to "Author's Suggested Readings" – please take a look at page 214. With regard to your two suggestions: (1) Reincarnation is controversial and whether one believes in it or not is not important per Jesus in ACIM – I took out my references/opinions on this subject in both Gary Renard's chapter (Chapter 8) and in my "Chat with Jesus" chapter (Chapter 9); and (2) You commented to me when we met that you thought my book needed something about 'overcoming the ego's arguments' as I recall - What I did was to strengthen the section entitled "<u>The Last Hurdle – Overcoming my Individuality</u>" contained on pages 157 and 158 of my book draft. Please let me know if this is good enough in your expert opinion.

My hope is that once you've reviewed this draft, we can have a phone conversation during which I can hear your comments. Also, I don't know how to get Gary Renard's okay to quote from his two books – perhaps you can give me a little direction on this? Anyway, I'll give you a holler in about a week by telephone and see what happens.

Was it the mad hatter or his tea party buddy who also confused *fasnarvitz* with *tzimmisses*? I don't recall. What comes to mind, however, is that you spell Mississippi as follows: "MISS ISS IPPI" and I dare any English speaking person to dispute this.

Can I forgive you for not endorsing my book? Since I made you up (and I'm really glad I did because you've made my dream a lot more interesting and fun), I have to forgive you to forgive me so I can awaken from this dream I still think I'm in.

Are you really crazier than me? Perhaps you are ….. Ummmm….

Anyway, I hope you won't be stuck at a funeral next month. We both know that there's no death anyway so can't you just "not go" on the basis that you don't believe in death anymore. Perhaps you ought to go only when you'll be raising someone from the dead. If Jesus is our example – and he's a good one you'll agree – my recollection is that the Bible only refers to 2 funerals that Jesus attended. One was his buddy, Lazarus, and Jesus brought him back to life. The other was his own funeral (the crucifixion, etc.) and 2 days later he walked away from that one, raising himself from the dead you might say. Anyway, whether or not you'll be at a funeral, only time will tell (even though time doesn't exist).

I Love you too, Brother Ken,

Jimmy "the hat" Laws

Copy – Tesha Laws
Attached-Draft Book dated May 14, 2012

<u>Ken Wapnick letter dated June 4, 2012</u>

Dear Jimmy the Hat,

That's the email address I have, too. Sorry. See you whenever, my friend. It's those damn funerals – people die at the most inappropriate times.

Love,

Ken

P.S. Give it up, Jimmy. You'll never be crazier than me! (You won't even be crazier than I!)

<u>Jimmy Laws letter dated August 13, 2012</u>

Dear Miracle Ken,

I hope this letter finds you and Gloria in a happy spiritual condition. Please tell her I said "hi" and I'm glad her sister's in good shape.

As for Tesha, Jimesha and I, we returned from a 2-1/2 week driving vacation 8 days ago and had a wonderful time. We spent 11 days in the Virginia Beach area where my son lives with his wife. My daughter from my first marriage flew down from Massachusetts with her husband for a long weekend while we were there so I had all 3 of my kids in one place for a while. From Virginia Beach, we drove to Greenville, South Carolina to spend 3 days with friends who moved there from our neighborhood about two years ago. The last leg of our journey was at the Florida State 12-Step Convention where there were about 2,500 attendees with many meetings and workshops – tremendous fun for all (or nearly all) who attended.

I believe Jesus has told me in his ACIM book that I'm still a beginner. You see, I still use words in my mind to try and stay spiritually focused. "Words can be helpful, <u>particularly for the beginner</u>, in helping concentration and facilitating the exclusion, or at least the control, of extraneous thoughts." [M-21.1.8] (emphasis added) As far as I know, I'm progressing nicely but if you have any helpful suggestions for me, please let me know.

I have put together a short series of thoughts to go to a Holy Instant quite quickly and have put it in writing for Tesha's benefit with some explanatory comments. I've been using it frequently throughout the day. I'm sharing it with you because you might find it helpful. It is as follows:

<u>QUICK HOLY INSTANT</u>

[1] This Holy Instant would I give to you, Jesus. Be you in charge. For I would follow you, certain that your direction gives me peace.

[2] God grant me peace.

[3] I am not a body. I am free for I am still as God created me. Above the battleground, I am determined to see.

[4] Help me Jesus. Help me Holy Spirit. Help me Christ. Help me Father. Help me Truth.

[5] Peace to my mind. Let all my thoughts be still.

[6] Let every voice but Yours be still in me.

[7] Forgiveness is the only gift I give.

[8] God is in everything I "see" because God is in my mind.

Explanation:

Naturally, we start here on earth (in our dream). The purpose of a Holy Instant (H.I.) is to take us out of our dream of space and time (the battleground), if only for a few seconds, to see our true reality, or to Truth.

Truth can also be defined by the words: Heaven, Allness, One Mind, Eternal Bliss, Love, Oneness, etc. Truth can also be defined by God plus His Creation (Christ plus the Holy Spirit).

Remember that God has given Himself to His Creation and the only difference between God and us is that God created us and we didn't create Him.

So we start on earth (the battleground) and we want to go to a H.I. so we ask for help as we move up the spiritual ladder from Jesus, to the Holy Spirit, to Christ, to our Father and to Truth (or eternal One-Mindedness). At this point, any earthly thoughts should be essentially gone and [5] and [6] help us stay here for a few seconds or more.

With [7] and [8], we come back down the ladder into our dream. Forgiveness, when lived, means to stay aware that everything I see with my eyes, hear with my ears, etc., was actually made up by my mind and so is a massive illusion made up by me – it is not real. In [8], I put quotes around the word see because, in this case, the word means what we see with our eyes whereas the Course generally uses see to mean vision - ignore the illusions of our eyes and see the eternal spirit underlying all things.

I had what I think is a major breakthrough this past Wednesday. This actually started Tuesday night when I really got verbally angry at Tesha. Naturally, I was wrong – anytime I'm even slightly annoyed, I'm wrong. During my quiet time early Wednesday morning, my Inner Voice (Jesus/Holy Spirit) suggested I stop ingesting caffeine into my system reminding me that all my angry outbursts since I've been clean and sober (15 years) have been when I've been highly caffeinated. The result has been I'm caffeine free starting Wednesday of last week. Tesha and I (as well as little Jimesha) are all on solid and happy spiritual ground today. (I logically commented to Tesha that if you marry a manic-depressive addict/alcoholic you can't really expect totally smooth sailing for the rest of your life. She understands intuitively that this recent incident was just a forgiveness opportunity for her. Just to be safe, however, I got some flowers for her yesterday☺.)

My book is moving along. I feel very fortunate that a well known publisher of spiritual books is critiquing my book (I sent him $1,500 for his fee for this) and will then likely publish it for me. He indicated his critique will be completed by early October and then some work will be required by me – I'm looking forward to the educational process of learning how to write a book which will appeal to the masses as I have a number of other books in mind.

*   *   *   *   *   *

Jesus Christ! Enough of this serious stuff! Let's get on with a little silliness, whadda say?

What a guy you are! You apparently took my advice and didn't attend any funerals during your June teaching sessions. I figure one of two things – (1) Being able to do things even greater than Jesus because of how spiritual you are, you raised those who died from the dead so there was no longer any need for the funerals, or (2) Knowing that the wonderful Jimmy the hat would be at your teaching sessions, you said the hell with the funerals☺ LOL☺.

Okay, now for a joke. When we were drinking, we drunks weren't too smart although we always thought we were. For example, these two drunks were driving along drinking beer when they saw a sobriety checkpoint ahead. They pulled over before the checkpoint, peeled the labels off their beer bottles and slapped the labels on their foreheads. When they then pulled up to the checkpoint and the cop asked them if they'd been drinking they replied: "Why no officer. We're on the patch." LOL ☺ LOL!

Oh yeah, Tesha really likes you – before she met you in June, she only really knew you through our letters which I shared with her. What a surprise to her – you come across as a rationale human being in front of an audience. Anyway, if she comes back in a future lifetime, I'm sure she'll be looking to marry a Jew from Brooklyn whose a prominent teacher of ACIM – that's how much you impressed her.

I Love you too, Brother Ken,

Jimmy "the hat" Laws

Copy – Tesha Laws

Ken Wapnick letter dated August 16, 2012

Dear Jimmy the Hat,

Nice to hear from you, you silly guy, you. And nice to hear that you are alive, well, and as preposterously silly as ever.

It was lovely having you all here and I'm glad I was able to meet St. Tesha. You had better hold on to her. And do tell her that I liked her very much, but am still working on liking her *ferschlugginer*[1] husband!

Keep writing, my friend, and keep on keeping your hat on.

Love to you, Tesha and Jimesha. And I look forward to your next visit in ten years.

Love,

Ken

[1]A Yiddish word meaning 'an old battered piece of junk.' LOL! LOL!

<u>Jimmy Laws letter dated September 19, 2012</u>

Dear Miracle Ken,

I hope the world you made up is looking brighter and brighter just as mine is.

Thank you very much for your excellent voice mail answer to my question. I just spent about 15 seconds standing on my left foot without a hat on and, would you believe, it just doubled my level of spirituality? You are a spiritual giant, Ken! LOL ... LOL ... LOL. Actually, you are a great mentor to me and I feel so privileged and blessed to have you take a personal interest in me. Thank you so very much.

A very significant thing happened to me recently. As a result of a suggestion from my Inner Voice (Jesus/Holy Spirit), I've ingested no caffeine into my body since August 7th. This has had a very positive impact on me – Tesha agrees.

Meanwhile, Tesha is attending GED classes every school day, from 8 am 'til 12 noon, in our local town and is really enjoying it – She's a "happy learner".

Your simple statement during one of your sessions regarding that great question from Jimmy the hat was the material in the URTEXT which was not included in the published version was because it came from Helen's ego and not from Jesus was most important for me to know. I had thought I knew more than the average Course student because of my study of the URTEXT. I've been doing my best to erase some of the nonsense I had absorbed and found it really helps so thank you for that little gem.

For the first time in a few years, I've been attending an ACIM study group which meets every two weeks and I'm really enjoying it. When I attended these in the past, I didn't enjoy them very much because my ego was telling me I'm too advanced for most ACIM students.

My publisher should have his report on my AA/ACIM book within the next few weeks. Then I'll have some work to do to polish up my book. I'm looking forward to it.

I'm waking up from my dream but it takes time – which isn't even real – so go figure.

        I Love you Brother Ken,

Jimmy "the hat" Laws

Copy – Tesha Laws

A footnote to my readers regarding caffeine: My "no caffeine" experiment was short lived. I'm back to drinking quite a bit of it.

<u>Ken Wapnick letter dated September 24, 2012</u>

Dear Jimmy the Hat,

How could your world look brighter? I thought it was already bright, and didn't you teach me that there is no hierarchy of brightness. You silly trickster, you!

No caffeine? That must make you pretty dull, boring, and unexciting. Are you sure that Tesha likes you that way? Speaking of whom, please give the angel a big hug for me.

And what is this about *my* book. You have the most annoying way of worming your way into things that are not your concern. But you were probably testing me to see if I were paying attention to you. So, did I pass?

Keep giggling, and stop being so damn serious about things, especially "your" book!

Love,

Ken

<u>Jimmy Laws letter dated November 9, 2012</u>

Dear Miracle Ken,

We are really busy. Jimesha just turned 5 and we're having a big birthday party at our house on Sunday – there'll probably be about 100 people over. It will be great fun. (I often get so busy that I forget I'm not here but I'm sure that's okay, don't you think?)

Meanwhile, I've completed the homework assigned to me by my publisher. I've attached a copy of his outline for the 12-Step/ACIM book with a lot of restructuring and rewriting suggested. Also attached is my follow-up to his suggestions, dated November 8, 2012. (I think you might really like the "12 steps of ACIM" listed in Part 2 of my letter – I do!) If you get a chance to look at this stuff and have any suggestions for me, please don't hesitate to let me know.

I sure hope you and I, at least, can have a meal together when I'm out there in March – Tesha won't be with me primarily because Jimesha has school.

Thanks for sharing part of my dream with me.

Oh yeah, "God bless you, my friend".

I Love you Brother Ken,

Jimmy "the hat" Laws

Attachments: My publisher's letter to me-9/24/12; My response-11/8/12
Copy – Tesha Laws

Ken Wapnick letter dated November 14, 2012

Dear Jimmy the pain-in-the-hat Hat,

Sounds like you may just have a book after all. Far out! You did good on your homework assignment. Don't stop!

As for a meal in March, do you really think I eat during those classes? What kind of spiritual dud do you think I am? And I don't believe that you eat then. You're putting me on, right?

Wish Jimesha a happy birthday for me, along with a hug. And while you're at it, one for St. Tesha. And if you insist, you can have one too!

Love,

Ken

Dear Miracle Ken,

Thank you for your November 14th letter and your continued encouragement on this book "you've gotten me into."

I've attached a copy of my publisher's latest response and my follow-up homework correspondence back to him. He asked me to simplify the 12 steps of ACIM which I did. I also told him why we can't use the term "12 steps" but can refer to them as "12 principles from ACIM."

It's not a big deal for me but do you want me to email future "book correspondence" to you? (I know you told me you didn't do personal email but this is a little different.)

As for the meal in March, of course I was thinking about doing that either before or after the week you'll be teaching. (Naturally I fast during all the days that you teach, whether I'm there in California or here in Florida – Doesn't every good ACIM student fast on days when "Miracle Ken" is teaching? ☺)

Thanks for the hugs which I passed on to Saint Tesha and Jimesha.

Thank you for your continued motivation and direction. By the way, my voice mail message no longer refers to me as "Jimmy the hat" and it was your influence that caused me to change that. But what do you think? Should I change it back? ☺

I'll take this opportunity to wish you, Gloria and your family and friends a

real Happy Thanksgiving.

I Love you Brother Ken,

Jimmy "the hat" Laws

Attachments: My publisher's letter to me-11/13/12; My response-11/18/12
Copy – Tesha Laws

Ken Wapnick letter dated November 27, 2012

Dear Jimmy the What??????????????????,

Thanks for keeping me in your publisher's loop. Does that mean you think I'm loopy?

It's hard for me to make definite plans this far in advance, but lunch before or after the March Academy sounds do-able. Of course if it's after, you may want to rethink having anything to do with me. I know for a fact that I shall be in one helluva rotten mood that week.

Yeah, I would stick with being hatless on your voice mail. Just make sure you shampoo your hair first. And if you insist, you can email me on your book stuff: eas.facim@gmail.com. God are you ever impossible! Would starting to drink again help, do you think? It's either that or you will drive me to drink!

Love,

Ken

Jimmy Laws letter dated December 14, 2012

Dear Miracle Ken,

Thank you for your November 27th letter.

I've attached a copy of my publisher's latest response and my follow-up homework correspondence back to him. He emailed me back indicating he likely wouldn't respond until after the 1st of the year because of all the holiday activities. In turn, I emailed him back saying that really works for me because I've been as busy as a "one armed paper hanger."

I love the question you asked me – Do I think you're loopy? I think you think you're in a make believe world. You think that you and our Father are one. You think that guys like Hitler and Bin Laden are no different than you or me or Mother Theresa or Jesus. You think there is no death. Virtually every psychiatrist in the world would have you put away for a long time if you shared this with him or her. Instead, through your books and lectures, you're trying to teach others this same insanity. Are you loopy? Of course you are! Of course, since I agree with this same insane thinking (by worldly standards), I'm loopy too.

Now, I want to talk to you about being honest, okay? Regarding the teaching week you'll have in March, you said "I know for a fact that I shall be in one helluva rotten mood that week." I'm quite convinced this is not true. I don't believe you've been in a rotten mood for many a year and you're just "pulling my leg", right? Or perhaps knowing that I'll be there that week is causing you a lot of grief? [You said that I'll drive you to drink which gives me a great idea! If I drive you to drink enough, you'll start drinking alcoholically and you can join a 12-step program and I can be your sponsor – Won't that be grand? LOL! LOL!]

Well, I'm really looking forward to seeing you that week and also having a meal with you. Please note that my publisher indicated he might try and be there for these classes which would give me a chance to meet him.

Meanwhile, Tesha and Jimesha are doing real good even though they have to put up with me. Please tell Gloria I said hi and I pray for her a whole lot because she has to put up with a "super loopy" husband like you.

I Love you Brother Ken,

Jimmy "the hat" Laws

Attachments: My letter to my publisher dated 11-18-12 with his comments in red type; My response-12-9-12
Copy – Tesha Laws

Dear Jimmy the Hat,

God, are you ever the royal pain-in-the-hat hat! And what is all this about twelve this and twelve that? You do know, I hope, that Jesus can't count past *one*. So what is all this complication? You always lose me once you get past the first whatever the hell you call it.

But no matter, Jimmy the royal pain-in-the-hat Hat, if you give your book a flashy cover it might find a place in my bookcase. Form is everything, you know, as long as the content remains *one*.

As for our March meal together, we had it already. Remember? You spilled stuff all over your hat, remember now? Anyway, I hope you're not one of those strange ones who believe time is linear, and that what has already happened is yet to come.

One final question, do you take off your hat when you shower? Love to dear Tesha and sweet Jimesha. And if there is any left over, some love for you too.

Love,

Ken

P.S. Kenneth will be out of the office beginning Thursday December 20th and will return on Thursday January 3rd. Unfortunately he will be unable to respond to any letters written during this time until he has returned to the office.

<u>Jimmy Laws letter dated January 26, 2013</u>

Dear Miracle Ken,

Thanks for asking me to do this paper on ACIM's special function.

It's possible I've "missed the boat" on this. However, I'm sure you'll let me know and you'll see how screwed up I still am – I hope you don't give up on me though?

Tesha, Jimesha and I are all real happy most of the time.

Please say hi to Gloria for me.

Your Florida buddy,

Jimmy Laws

P.S. I'm dropping "the hat" when I introduce myself at 12-step meetings. I'm making progress.

Attachment – My "Special Function" paper

<u>This is the attachment to my January 26, 2013 letter to Ken</u>

To: Ken Wapnick   January 26, 2013

From: Since I reference my 12-step membership herein, I wish to remain anonymous so you can share this with others if you see any value.

Background: After 14 years of rigorous study of ACIM, I thought I knew what "Chapter 25.VI. The Special Function" meant. So I asked you if your "Special Function" was to teach ACIM during your life.

Your response included the following thoughts. Your special function has nothing to do with your profession (of teaching ACIM). You said your special function was the same as mine, indicating that I had totally misunderstood what this part of ACIM was saying. If your special function were different than mine, you said, then you would be "different than" me rather than "the same as" me. [We know that, in truth, there is only ONE Mind so there are, of course, no differences.]

Then you gave me this homework assignment – to explain what "Special Function" means – which is represented by this paper. (I hope you were kidding when you said it should be 10,000 words. It's only about 1,300 words.)

<u>This Paper: The Special Function [See ACIM T-25.VI.]</u>

There is one primary person in my life who I don't like very much. This is clearly (to me) my problem and not his. I'm going to use this man to define what I now think my special function is.

Please note that I am a very active member of a 12-step fellowship and have over 1,000 friends and acquaintances in my town and adjacent towns who are members of this fellowship as well as many other people in my life. With over 90% of those in my 12-step fellowship I get along great. Of the other 10%, Alabama Ron (not his real name) is the one I like the least and for a very good earthly reason – Alabama Ron doesn't really like me and historically he's been verbal about this. Even from pure earthly common sense, this shouldn't bother me at all because Ron doesn't like a lot of people and is verbal about them too. Therefore, I clearly shouldn't take Ron's dislike for me personally but I do. And, as I stated above, this is clearly my problem since I've brought Ron into my earthly dream.

To give you an idea of how I've allowed this to affect me, for the past couple of years I've avoided going to those 12-step meetings where Ron goes regularly. I have a fear that he'll say something to me which will cause me to get angry and perhaps even respond back to him with words I'll regret. There is only one other person in the whole 12-step fellowship which I allow to affect me. Note that the fear of these two men is not at all stifling and when I do see them I say hello cordially. However, since there is a wide variety of 12-step meetings available to me, I prefer going to meetings where I won't run into these two men.

As I've given this some serious thought as a result of this homework assignment, I think I want to be the best 12-stepper in our area and I reckon Ron wants this to be his claim to fame. Our ego has set this animosity up and I'm now quite convinced that I need to back down from this ego thinking and let the Holy Spirit in more.

My dislike (resentment or grievance) against Ron, I think, provides me with an opportunity for my Special Function.

Section VI of Chapter 25 talks of my special function as follows:

Paragraph 1 – This paragraph, to me, describes the persona of Jesus when he walked here in the dream world some 2,000 years ago.

Paragraph 2 – Tells me that my eyes are not yet fully opened. If they were then there is no way I would now be judging Alabama Ron at all. Intellectually, I know Ron is 100% innocent, eternal, the same as me, ONE with me, Jesus and everyone and all life, and is ONE with God now and forever and ever.

Paragraph 3 – In terms of Alabama Ron, this paragraph tells me God wants me to see him as eternally innocent (just as I am). The paragraph tells me Ron is my savior. God doesn't want Ron to continue with his negative attitude – God wants him to have the function of forgiveness which God gave him. The last part of the paragraph talks about Ron being lonely which, compared to where I'm at today, I'm quite convinced he is.

Paragraph 4 – The Holy Spirit wants me to allow Him (the Holy Spirit) to heal the relationship between Ron and me.

Paragraph 5 – With the Holy Spirit leading the way, I'm quite convinced this relationship between Ron and I will improve in the days to come.[1] I think of this as my special function at this time.

Paragraph 6 – I'd like to comment on one sentence in this paragraph: "His special sin was made his special grace." Here's how I interpret this: My "special sin", like everyone else in this dream world, was thinking that I'm separate from everyone else. My "special grace" includes my ability, with the ongoing guidance of the Holy Spirit and Jesus, to use my body as a wonderful communication device which ACIM tells us is its only purpose. Therefore, as guided by my Inner Voice (Holy Spirit/Jesus), the fractured relationship between Alabama Ron and I can be mended.

Paragraph 7 – In part, this paragraph reads as follows (I've added the words shown in parenthesis): "In light, you see it as your special function in the plan to save the Son of God from all attack, and let him (Alabama Ron and me) understand that he is safe, as he has always been, and will remain in time and in eternity alike. This is the function given you for your brother (Alabama Ron). Take it gently, then, from your brother's hand, and let salvation be perfectly fulfilled in you. Do this *one* thing, that everything be given you."

<u>From the "Concordance of ACIM", following are some other references to "special function"</u>:

T-25.VII.7:1 "Your special function is the special form in which the fact that God is not insane appears most sensible and meaningful to you."

T-25.VII.9:2 "To each his special function is designed to be perceived as possible, and more and more desired, as it proves to him that it is an alternative he really wants." (i.e., to get along good with Alabama Ron.)

T-25.VII.9:6 "He can no more be left outside, without a special function in the hope of peace, than could the Father overlook His Son, and pass him by in careless thoughtlessness." (Of course I hope for peace in my mind regarding my relationship with Alabama Ron.)

T-25.VII.12:7 and T-25.VII.12:8 As I read these two sentences, both Ron and I gain, of course, if our relationship goes from adversarial to friendly.

T-25.VIII.11:5 As I read this sentence, the Holy Spirit allotted me this Alabama Ron special relationship so that both he and I can benefit from it.

T-25.VIII.12:5 My special function is simply a call to the Holy Spirit to have Him repair my insane thinking with regard to Alabama Ron. With regard to any action on my part in my dream, I will do my best to accomplish the following: "I will step back and let Him lead the way."

T-25.VIII.14:3 "Your special function shows you nothing else but perfect justice can prevail for you." (i.e., I'm 100% innocent and so is Alabama Ron.)

T-26.I.5:2 "Without your special function has this world no meaning for you." This suggests my special function is ongoing, not simply reconciling with Alabama Ron. However, I can always find some new lonely and/or angry person to befriend.

T-26.I.8:4 and T-26.I.8:5 These 2 sentences reinforce my thinking that if I can help Alabama Ron and me to be friends, it will really help him (as well as me).

T-26.II.6:5 Here again is reference to my relationship with someone else.

T-26.II.8:4 "Your special function opens wide the door beyond which is the memory of His Love kept perfectly intact and undefiled."

T-26.III.7:1 "Is not this like your special function, where the separation is undone by change of purpose in what once was specialness, and now is union?" This sentence certainly coincides with me reconciling with Alabama Ron.

---

[1] I am very pleased to tell you readers of this book that my relationship with Alabama Ron has improved very significantly since this paper was written, over 4 years ago.

<u>Ken Wapnick letter dated January 30, 2013</u>

Dear Jimmy the What???????,

You did good with your "assignment." All I would add is that you look at how much you do *not* want to forgive the bastard. Look at Jesus' message to Helen and Bill on pages 297-98 in my *Absence from Felicity*, and the beginning of T-13.III.

Okay now, get busy!!!! Send my love to St. Tesha and sweet Jimesha, and you too, I guess.

Love,

Ken

To: Ken Wapnick

From: Since I reference my 12-step membership herein, I wish to remain anonymous so you can share this with others if you see any value.

Re: "Special Function" homework assignment

Dear Miracle Ken:

I received your January 30, 2013 letter. Thank you very much.

As it turns out, a week before I received your letter I was at a 12-step business meeting with Alabama Ron and about 8 other people. Although Ron picked on me a little bit, I was *virtually* undisturbed by him and I thought we got along quite good. It's clear to me the internal work I had done and summarized in writing to you on 1-26-13 helped me a lot.

I did read the passages you asked me to read (discussed below).

In my ongoing study of ACIM, I recently finished the full ACIM again, including the 2 supplements [Psychotherapy and Song of Prayer], so I started reading from the beginning once again. When I got to page 3 of the Text, I decided to read your book, *The 50 Miracle Principles of ACIM,* rather than just speed read through what I think is the most difficult part of the Course. Though I had read your "50" book some years back, it has been much more meaningful with this go round. Thank you, Ken, for an excellent job.

I. Some Babbling by me

I want to ask you about something else thinking there's a good chance you've crossed this hurdle yourself. At this point in time, my most priceless personal relationship is that between Jimesha [our 5-year old daughter] and me. It is, of course a "special" relationship to me but I believe it is also a Holy relationship. [Tesha, my wife, is my second in line as a "special" Holy relationship.]

A concern I have is that if I remove all the barriers between me and God [i.e., listen only to the Holy Spirit/Jesus and never to my ego] then God will "take me home" before I get to see Jimesha grow up and be here physically for her. In general, life here on earth is becoming so wonderful, I don't want to leave.

This really sounds like a stupid question but here it is: Should I slow down in my ACIM studies so I delay the time of my body's cessation?

On another note, I'd like to mention here the "You are me" mental tool I frequently use. Using "Alabama Ron" as an example [or "the bastard" as you've described him – LOL], when I see him as less worthy than me [I judge him], that is clearly an attack by me on him as attack is defined in the Course. In truth, we are all equal and we are all One since God only has One Son which ACIM calls Christ. When I pass people in a store, I often say the mental phrase "You are me" which helps me a lot. It especially reduces or eliminates my lust defect with regard to very beautiful women. So to Alabama Ron I say "You are me" since God only has One Son with One Mind [which God and the Holy Spirit share with us].

II. Pages 297-98 in your *Absence from Felicity*

There is, of course, some real relevance to me and my relationship with Alabama Ron concerning what Jesus told Bill and Helen on September 13th and 14th, 1966:

(1) "You do not realize how much you hate each other. You will not get rid of this until you do realize it, for until then, you will think you want to get rid of each other and keep the hatred." [As I alluded to in my last letter, I have been avoiding the weekly 12-step meeting which Ron goes to regularly. I've been avoiding Ken but keeping the hatred.]

(2) "Yet if you are each other's salvation, what can this mean except that you *prefer* attack to salvation?" Ron is, of course, my savior, as is every other human being I meet. Currently, Ron is probably my greatest teacher.

As I noted at the beginning of this letter, when I recently was at a business meeting with Ron, I was *virtually* undisturbed by him. However, I was not 100% undisturbed by him. This means that I am still holding on to some fear or grievance or attack thoughts or ..... against Ron. It's my understanding that Jesus teaches many times in ACIM that the difference between, say, a small annoyance at someone and absolute screaming in hatred is zero (-0-). I think Jesus is telling me that, either way, my ego is still directing my mind. Is this accurate thinking? In any event, I still have some work to do on me with the help of the Holy Spirit and Jesus and one of their greatest emissaries in the world today, a man called Ken Wapnick. Thank you very much for your help, Miracle Ken.

I, of course, know that Alabama Ron is the same as me when I simply step back and use Christ's Vision.

By the way, I think Ron and I could smooth out our relationship a lot quicker if he were a solid student of ACIM and I could share all this stuff with him. [Although I've never asked him, I'm quite convinced he's not an ACIM student.] He actually thrives on grievances and historically braggingly shares that there are many people in our 12-step fellowship who he doesn't like. By the way, he's been clean from drugs and alcohol for about 25 years.

III. ACIM T-13.III

T-13.III.2.2 - "For this memory would instantly restore you to your proper place, and it is this place that you have sought to leave."

T-13.III.2.6 – "You realize that, by removing the dark cloud that obscures it, your love for your Father would impel you to answer His Call and leap into Heaven."

T-13.III.3.3 – "For you could not control your joyous response to the call of love if you heard it, and the whole world you thought you made would vanish."

T-13.III.4.3 – "You think you made a world God would destroy; and by loving Him, which you do, you would throw this world away, which you *would.*"

Taken literally, Jesus says how we will instantly leave our dream world and leap Home to Heaven once all our ego barriers are overcome.

Despite a few "bastards" in my life like Alabama Ron, there is no way I want to leave my dream for a long time especially in consideration of Jimesha, our little five-year old. In Principle 24 of your book *The 50 Miracle Principles of ACIM* you said: "The goal (of ACIM) is to change the nightmare dream into a happy dream." This has happened for me even though I'm not yet egoless.

o   o   o   o   o

I think the answer to my dilemma comes from Arten and Pursah's significant other relationship which they had in their last lifetime. Pursah became enlightened [or egoless] before Arten but she hung around for a number of years in the dream world so it wouldn't be as painful to Arten when she "died". Thus, it appears if I become egoless later tonight, I can hang around for another 37 years [I'd then be 100] or so if I want to. I sure hope I can still smoke cigarettes during these remaining years without any ill effects 'cause I really like them.

The review of the above sections has really helped me so thank you Ken for asking me to do this.

Please note that I'll be flying in to California on March 7th and returning home on March 26th. [Tesha and Jimesha will not be with me.] I sure hope we can get together during one of the weekdays I'm there for a meal or something – I'm buying! If we can't, I'm still very much looking forward to seeing you at your teaching sessions during the week of March 11th.[1]

God bless you, Ken. Why did I say that? Did you sneeze?

[1] I was able to have an hour long lunch with Ken during this trip. What a privilege for me!

Ken Wapnick letter dated February 14, 2013

Dear Jimmy,

Boy did you get this wrong (must be that hat you are no longer wearing). When your mind is healed *you do not necessarily die.* One thing has nothing to do with the other. All that will change is that you will stop being so obstreperous (even if you don't know how to pronounce or spell it). Okay, I'm glad we got that straight.

Sounds like you are doing real well with dear Ron. Just keep going as you are going. But don't work so hard at this. Nothing upsets Jesus more than hard workers! Be easy, be gentle, be silly.

Call me when you get into town, and then we'll see what kinds of excuses I come up with so as not to see you.

Love,

Ken

P.S. Have no fear, Jesus doesn't care if you smoke as long as you don't blow the smoke in his face.

February 28, 2013

Dear Miracle Ken,

Thank you for taking my phone call on Tuesday – The ACIM group that I attended was very good and I "had fun" as you instructed me to.

Also, thank you for your letter of February 14th. What a great word "obstreperous" is after I looked up its definition, having no idea what it meant. My dictionary says it means "noisy and refusing to do what someone asks." So you told me to stop being noisy and refusatory. Both of these brought to mind Jesus' teachings or ideas from ACIM as I recall. He tells us that if someone asks us to do something we should just do it without thinking (unless to do so would hurt one of us). Somewhere he says that a person who really "gets it" can change the world even though he or she never utters a word – perhaps I misinterpreted this? Clearly, Jesus communicated verbally to a lot of people, I talk to a lot of people and certainly you do too.

I found I'm a successful author – pretty neat, eh? About 7 years ago, I self-published a book on the LULU.COM website which was a workbook to help 12-step students work the 12 steps. It's only 36 pages long and I used a pen name (for anonymity reasons). As I'm considering the self-publishing of the book you reviewed, I went back to my old LULU.COM account and found not only that a whole bunch of people bought the book but that LULU owed me money on it. They recently sent us a check for a little over a thousand bucks. I hope money and fame don't cause my ego to grow any bigger than it already is – I've seen it happen to others but I really have no fear for myself.

I am so looking forward to your March classes and my time in California. Since I arrive late on Thursday, March 7th, I'll call you on Friday. I'll be there in California until March 26th. I sure hope we can spend some "social" time together – I know it will be fun and perhaps we can talk about a future book called "Silly Spirituality" or some such fun title.

God bless you Ken – you've sneezed at some time I reckon – LOL,

Jimmy Laws

P.S. Please tell Gloria I said hi and Jimesha is going to want a full report on the Pooh Bear she gave you some time ago.

Ken Wapnick letter dated April 8, 2013

Dear Jimmy the What??????????,

Sweet card, lovely picture, but what the hell did you mean about no payment? Wait until you get my bill!!!!!!!!!!!!!!!!!!!!!

Love,

Ken

P.S. Kenneth will be out-of-town beginning Thursday April 18th through Monday April 29th. Unfortunately he will be unable to respond to any letters you may write during this time until after having returned to the office.

<u>Jimmy Laws letter dated April 30, 2013</u>

Dear Miracle Ken,

How is Gloria? I hope the people in Texas were able to help her. Please let her know my prayers have been reaching out to her (and you, too, my good friend).

As you suggested, I signed up for your November classes shortly after I returned home and I now have a reservation for spending another week with you ...... and I'm really looking forward to it. I gain so much every time I sit through your sessions.

Meanwhile, I've been busy. In my February 28th letter, I mentioned I was a successful author on a 12-step workbook. Well, I've since updated that book and have enclosed a copy for your perusal and library. I used the self-publishing LULU.COM website to accomplish this.

Now, I'm commencing to get my 12-Step/ACIM book out also using LULU.COM. My hope is to get this out by the end of May when Tesha, Jimesha and I head to Guyana for two months.

I have also completed my latest homework assignment from you – I've read your two volumes from *The Message of A Course in Miracles* and found they helped me a lot so thank you for this assignment. Here are just a few of the things which hit home for me:

1. As you did in your March classes, you emphasized me as the decision maker: I'll choose either the ego or the Holy Spirit/Jesus. I need only choose the Holy Spirit/Jesus – How simple is that?

2. I really liked these alternate thoughts: "The miracle says look inside for the solution whereas magic says look outside for the solution."

3. You've helped solidify this simple statement: "'There is no world' is ACIM's central thought."

4. I liked this thought: "Never pray for illusions to replace illusions."

5. I got this idea when reading these volumes: "Love is not a thinking thing." [e.g., During our Holy Instant experiences or experiencing the "peace of God that passes all understanding", there is no

thinking.| So I guess it can be said that "Thinking is outside God's Will." What do you think – LOL?

I'll answer this – As Jesus says in his Course, we must "unlearn" what we were convinced was real (e.g., the world) and we, of course, must unlearn it with the help of the Holy Spirit/Jesus. This, it seems to me, requires thinking. Another way to put this is: "We thought our way into this insane world and, with the help of God (Jesus/Holy Spirit), we have to think our way out of it."

6. On page 87 of *Few Choose to Listen*, you recommend the reading and re-reading of ACIM which I've been doing for 14-plus years now and I can attest that this really works. I must say, however, that I've never heard you make this recommendation during any of your classes. Perhaps you do recommend it and I've just been day dreaming or thinking about my next joke – LOL?

7. I really liked your definition of "content" when you discussed the difference between content and form. Everyone's "content" is "100% eternal innocent spirit". (All form, of course, is just illusion.)

My general plan is to continue to write books. I enjoy this avocation also, as you said you do.

Meanwhile, however, do you have any more reading assignments for me at this point in time?

* * * * * * * *

I want to leave you with a joke which you should share with others so you can remember it:

Q – What do you call a dog with no legs?

A – It doesn't matter what you call him. He's not going to come anyway. LOL! LOL!

* * * * * * * *

God bless you my good friend. Please tell Gloria and the staff there at your offices that I said hi.

Jimmy "the hat" Laws

Enclosed: My revised 12-Step Workbook

Dear Jimmy the Who?,

Your revised edition looks really good.

Now that you have read "The Message of *A Course in Miracles*," read it again. This time come up with nine home-hitting things instead of seven.

You are one helluva piece of work. Keep writing! By the way, I don't know why you want to come here in November. I'm already in a rotten mood thinking of that class.

Love,

Ken

P.S. Gloria was really helped by her surgery. Thank you for your kind thoughts.

<u>Jimmy Laws letter dated May 28, 2013</u>

Dear Miracle Ken,

Thank you for your letter of May 3rd. I'm, of course, real glad to hear that Gloria was helped by her surgery. Please tell her I said hi.

Thank you, also, for complimenting me on the 12-Step workbook I sent you.

I was hoping to get my 12-Step/ACIM book – the one you reviewed a long time ago – published before we left for Guyana (May 29th, tomorrow) but I ran into some technical problems and have run out of time. I now hope to get it published while I'm in Guyana and I think I can have a copy mailed to you while I'm there – I don't expect to be back in the U.S.A. until the end of July.

In the updated book, I have left out the chapter on my manic depressive illness and the Gary Renard promotional chapter. A significant change in the rest of the book is basically changing the words "my ego" to "the ego" throughout the book. I learned this from the recent classes I attended out there with you. This has been real helpful to me and simplified this whole deal in my mind: "There are only two voices available to all people in this dream world – (1) The one we all start with and believe which is the ego's voice (or Satan's if one prefers) which tells us of separation, pleasure, pain, good times and bad times, suffering, friends, enemies, and, of course, death; and (2) The Voice of Truth – the Voice of Jesus/Holy Spirit – which tells us of the dream/nightmare we think we're in and, through the mind training of ACIM (for many of us who choose ACIM), the guarantee of awakening to eternal life for all of us back to the Oneness of God and His Creation."

I plan on reading "The Message of *A Course in Miracles*" again while I'm in Guyana. I'm also hoping to start on my third book while I'm there – Perhaps my pen name will become a famous name within the next few years. LOL!

I've got an idea which should really help you get excited about your November classes. Just be a little open minded here, Ken. This will really put *ACIM* and Ken Wapnick "on the map". The Foundation announces well in advance that on the afternoon of November 15th, Ken Wapnick, leading teacher of *A Course in Miracles* in the world, will be "ascending towards Heaven" and all are invited. This should generate a lot of publicity – probably even worldwide.

"How is this to be accomplished?" you're probably asking. First, you must keep this a secret but it's real simple. Let's suppose a helium balloon (all 'Dollar Tree' stores in the U.S. sell them) can lift 0.2 lbs. (we can find the exact number and adjust the balloon count accordingly if you like my idea) and let's say you weigh 180 lbs. with your clothes on, including the weight of your harness (to which the balloons will be attached) and your balloon popper (which you'll need to get back down to the ground). This means we'll need 900 balloons to offset your weight and perhaps another 100 balloons to give you some lift.

So picture the scene. Shortly after your last class on November 15th, you walk outside with your harness on holding your balloon popper in one hand – basically a stick with an ice pick at the end (I can bring duct tape to attach the ice pick). Immediately following you are 5 staff members, each holding 200 balloons which they attach to your harness. You wave to the huge crowd and kiss Gloria goodbye. Then your staff lets go of the balloons and you rise into the sky, ascending towards the heavens. Once you've drifted some, you start using your balloon popper so as to make sure you land on the Foundation's property (and not on the freeway).

The cheering crowd will applaud you! Worldwide publicity for you and *ACIM* will be guaranteed! Companies that sell helium and balloons will love you! What a great idea, eh? LOL!

God bless you my good friend.

Jimmy "the hat" Laws

Ken Wapnick letters dated May 31, 2013 and June 12, 2013

From my August 24th letter which follows, I know that Ken sent me these letters but I have since lost them – my apologies.

Dear Miracle Ken,

We returned home 23 days ago and one of my top agenda items has been to write this letter to you. I apologize for taking so long in doing this. I believe you've forgiven the world you made up so I therefore believe you've forgiven me.

Thank you for your letter of May 31st responding to my balloon idea. I often think of the world as a giant cartoon of my making and, of course, laying out that crazy idea for you was done for the "fun of it"! I like this acronym which, as far as I know, I invented: KISS which stands for "Keep It Silly Spiritually."

Also, thank you for your June 12th letter acknowledging receipt of my 12-Step/ACIM book and the "Good Job!" comment. Your encouragement helps me tremendously!

All 3 of us – Tesha, Jimesha and I had a wonderful time in Guyana. To give you a little idea, I've attached 4 emails I sent to friends and family. The last one is a poem I wrote to Tesha on our 7th wedding anniversary on June 15th. Lines 3 through 6 refer to the morning following the first time Tesha spent the night at my place, before we were married. Her older sister, Neeka, was so angry that she literally started beating Tesha physically with heavy blows. It is conceivable had I not physically dragged Neeka off of Tesha that Neeka could have killed her. We were living on St. Martin at the time. Shortly after this incident, Tesha's Mom (Mayleen) arrived unannounced on St. Martin for 8 days with only one purpose in mind – to break up the engagement between her youngest daughter and the old perverted white man (that would be me-smile). This is what lines 7 and 8 of the poem are about. Well, Mayleen didn't succeed and I'm happy to say that both Mayleen and Neeka are both very good friends of mine today.[1]

If you got to listen to the voice mail message I left you Sunday night, you know that Tesha is pregnant and I am the Daddy – Thank God for Viagra! We're all excited about this. Our little Jimesha, now 5, is hoping for twins or triplets or more. Importantly, we will be having this baby here in the U.S. and the plan is for Tesha to take it real easy during this entire pregnancy, as she did when she was pregnant with Jimesha. I don't know if you remember that in 2006 Tesha had a baby boy who was stillborn and in February, 2010 we had a little girl who died after about 2 months – her lungs never developed and she was in the hospital the whole time. Tesha's doing real good and we're real optimistic that all will go well with our new baby.[2]

Meanwhile, Jimesha started kindergarten this week and is really enjoying it – She gets on the school bus at 7 am and gets dropped off at 3 pm. She's a wonderful child and gets along with virtually everyone. You'll like this I expect – Jimesha believes that this life of hers is but a dream, that there is no death and that Jesus is with her all the time even though she can't see him. In other words, without any studying of ACIM, she believes its key principles and she's only 5 years old.

Starting on Tuesday of this week, Tesha and I are reading through the text of ACIM together for a little while each school day – no more than an hour. The plan is to continue this discipline every morning that Jimesha is in school.

Here's some great news too! While in Guyana, I started on my next book and it's pure ACIM. This means that when I finish it, I can use my real name which will be just "Jimmy Laws" and not "Jimmy 'the hat' Laws" – least wise, this is my current thinking. The book is straight forward, simply giving some of my own thoughts/experiences on each lesson from the Workbook and should be about 200 pages. While in Guyana, I was able to make a lot of progress and I could feel your inspiring voice saying "atta boy" to me as I was doing this. Life is a lot more complicated here at home so my progress has been delayed some but I hope to have the draft book completed by the time I see you again in November. Following is an introductory note I plan on including at the beginning of this book:

> "Any situation must be to you a chance to teach others what you are, and what they are to you. No more than that, but also never less." (M-Intro.2:10,11) This book is a situation for me, giving me an opportunity to teach those who read it who I am and what they are to me. In a nutshell, we are all travelers and our purpose is to save each other from this crazy dream we think we're in which we call the world. One of the key teachings from *A Course in Miracles* is that "every other person in the world is my savior" so thank you one and all, whether you read this book or not.[3]

I have one ACIM "technical" question for you regarding the question: What is our "special function?" Without going into all the mumbo jumbo verbiage, can't we just say that our special function is to turn any special relationships into holy relationships?[4]

I hope you and Gloria remain in good spirit.

God bless you my good friend.

Jimmy "the hat" Laws

Attachments – 4 emails

[1]Tesha, Mayleen (her mom), Neeka (her sister), me and many others laugh at all this today and very much enjoy telling the story to others.

[2]I am very happy to tell you that Jimmy Junior was born perfectly healthy on March 17, 2014 (St. Patrick's Day) and is doing great.

[3]This book was published in 2014. It's title is *Experiencing the Lessons of A Course in Miracles* by James R. Laws.

[4]Shortly after I mailed this letter, I was informed that Ken was hospitalized so I never got a response to this question from him. But I can now answer my own question quite well today. In the *Course*, Jesus spends a lot of time telling us of our special love and special hate relationships, all of which are 'sick' relationships. My special function is, with the help of Jesus of course, to have all my relationships become holy. My animosity towards Alabama Ron had been a special hate relationship for many years. As I've noted in previous letters, a lot of progress has been made on this. In "The Special Function" of the Text, Jesus tells me exactly what my purpose is in my relationship with Ron: "The Son of God can make no choice the Holy Spirit cannot employ on his behalf, and not against himself. Only in darkness does your specialness appear to be attack. In light, you see it as your special function in the plan to save the Son of God [Alabama Ron] from all attack, and let him understand that he is safe, as he has always been, and will remain in time and in eternity alike. This is the function given you [Jimmy] for your brother [Alabama Ron]." (T-25.VI.7:5-8)

End notes regarding my letters to and from Ken:

I received a letter dated August 7, 2013 from Ken's Assistant, Elizabeth Schmit indicating Ken had been hospitalized due to fluid in his pleura and he was resting comfortably but wouldn't be responding to letters for an indefinite time.

I received a letter dated October 3, 2013 from the FACIM Staff that the November Academy classes with Ken were being canceled so as to give Ken the time to heal and a refund of my tuition payment was forthcoming.

On December 27, 2013 Ken passed away.

Chapter 2: Duality as Metaphor in *A Course in Miracles*

This chapter consists of 2 sections as follows:

Section A: Introduction ….. Begins on this page.

Section B: My notes from "Duality as Metaphor" ….. page 166.

Section A: Introduction

This multiple day workshop was given to us by Ken Wapnick in October of 1993. I purchased this 11 hour CD disc set a few years back and have listened and learned from it on three separate occasions. It has become a very important addition to my ongoing study of the *Course*.

Approximately three months ago, as I was researching material for this book, I decided to listen to this workshop for the third time. Once again, I learned much from this last review and this section summarizes some of this new learning.

Before I do that, however, I want to share an epiphany I had during the second time I listened to this workshop, about a year ago, and where it has led me since.

First, however, I must tell you that very early in my *Course* studies, probably in 2000 when I had completed the Text, Workbook for Students and Manual for Teachers for the first time, I understood much of the basics. For instance, I understood that there is no death (only eternal life), everyone is already saved but we just don't know it, and the world's a dream and it's guaranteed that everyone will eventually wake up in Heaven. When thinking about these ideas and sometimes discussing them with others, my mind automatically went to Adolf Hitler as the most evil individual I could think of and I had no problem believing and knowing that he, like everyone else who ever lived, would at some point wake up in Heaven.

My habit when I listen to Ken's CDs is to listen to one and occasionally two CDs a day. So about a year ago, while simply sitting in my lanai during the week or so I had been listening to Ken's "Duality as Metaphor" CDs, I basically asked and answered the following question for the first time: Q- Where did Adolf Hitler come from? A-100% of Adolf Hitler and everything I know about him came from my mind. This was my epiphany - the realization that every single aspect of this separated world is 100% coming from my mind. It is literally no different from my night time dreams which clearly must come only from my mind.

This entire world of separation is <u>my</u> dream. The fact that in your own dream world you also have knowledge of Adolf Hitler and likely agree with my general opinion about the man does not change the fact that it's <u>my</u> dream I'm in. You have your own dream that you're in. If we ever meet someday, then you will then be in <u>my</u> dream. Meanwhile, this book that I've written is in your dream as it is also in mine.

I think the lesson which really explains this "<u>my</u> dream" idea is Lesson 139 – "I will accept Atonement for myself." I recall Ken telling me personally "Remember, Jimmy, you only have to accept Atonement for yourself."

This epiphany has really helped me with certain issues. For example, for many years I have had some prejudice against the religionist people who agree with the Bible without question. My pet peeve has been its description of a punishing God. With this epiphany I had, I can honestly say and know that I made up the Bible and the religionists who follow it because, quite simply, this whole world is but my dream. So if I get angry at religious people, I'm attacking <u>my</u> dream which is literally coming from my mind and therefore I'm clearly attacking myself.

Following are some of the other people or things I have made up:

1. If you've read my correspondence with Ken, you'll likely recall my special hate relationship with Arkansas Ron. Well, I made up Arkansas Ron.
2. I made up *A Course in Miracles*, and I'm really glad I did.
3. I made up Ken Wapnick, again real glad about this.
4. I made up Jesus, a most excellent illusion.
5. And, of course, I made up Jimmy Laws, the "hero" of my dream. (T-27.VIII is entitled "The 'Hero' of the Dream" and points this one out.)

To solidify this idea further, I like to share what Jesus tells us in Lesson 132: "There is no world! This is the central thought the course attempts to teach." (W-132.6:2-3) We can of course expand this to the following:

There never was a world!

There is no world now!

There won't be a world tomorrow!

These statements are literal truths. Jesus also tells us in the *Course* it will probably take millions of years before the entire Sonship wakes up from their dream worlds and awaken to the only reality which is Heaven and its oneness.

When I listened to Ken's very powerful 10-disc set again about a month ago, I gained even more insight into the *Course*. I plan on listening to it again and perhaps many more times. My own experience is that this particular workshop has been an extremely important addition to my ongoing study material.

Section B: My notes from "Duality as Metaphor"

The following reflect some of the notes I took while listening to the workshop three months ago:

1. Ken points out that the fear of losing our individuality will stop us from really benefiting from the *Course.*

    Here is a powerful simple sentence from the *Course*: *"Let me not forget myself is nothing, but my Self is all."* (W-358.1:7) Knowing that the word Self when used by Jesus in his *Course* means God's one and only Son (also defined as Christ), this literal statement means Jimmy Laws is, in fact, nothing but my true identity as Christ is everything. Although through the study of the *Course*, we can think of Heaven as comprised of the Creator, Christ and the Holy Spirit, we also learn that there is no separation whatsoever in the oneness of Heaven so we have all the power, glory, joy, peace, etc. that our Creator has without exception. The only difference between us and our Creator is that He created us and we didn't create Him.

    So suppose the ego were to say to me today: "You can't possibly want to give up your Jimmy Laws identity!" I might say: "Actually, Jimmy Laws is just an illusion you made up so, yes, I do want to give it up and eventually wake up at home in Heaven. However, before that happens, I know I have some work to do."

2. At one point in this workshop, Ken talks about studying the *Course* as something one does for a lifetime. For 18 years now, its study has become "a way of life" for me for the simple reason that I keep becoming ever more happy as a direct result of my studies. Up until the spring of 2013, I knew of no one else who studied the *Course* as much or as often as I did.

    In the spring of 2013, I was privileged to have lunch with Ken, just he and I. The most important question I asked him was: "Do you still study the *Course*?" Ken told me: "Yes, except when I'm writing books." In that answer Ken told me that I can "happily" expect to be studying the *Course* for the balance of time that the "Jimmy Laws" illusion continues on his illusionary world called "earth."

3. In the *Course* Jesus tells us many times that our only reality is Heaven where there is but One Mind. Thus, God plus Christ (His one Son) plus the Holy Spirit all have the same incredible, wonderful, joyful, eternal, happy, grateful, etc. Mind - the 3 of Us are literally one. You may recall from the *Course* that Jesus takes the Biblical quote "The kingdom of God is within you" and tells us we can simplify it to "The kingdom of God is you." Since "the kingdom of God" is a synonym for "Heaven", I can say "I am Heaven." Of course, so are you and so is everything else; Heaven is the only reality.

   There is, of course, no duality in Heaven, the Home from which we came and the home to which we will all return. In this workshop, Ken tells us a number of times: "Accept no compromise in which duality plays a part." What he means is that our minds should be set on the goal of Heaven which is 100% non-dualistic. Naturally, we are still moving along in our dream worlds which of course are dualistic. My understanding is that even when we have complete forgiveness (i.e., we have attained the real world) while living our dream life, we still won't experience Heaven until we lay our bodies down just as we would an old coat that has served its useful purpose.

4. Ken points out that much of what Jesus says in the *Course* should not be taken literally and he gives at least one example. He also tells us that some of the *Course* statements are to be taken literally and includes some of these throughout this workshop.

5. Chapter 12 of the Manual for Teachers asks: "How many teachers of God are needed to save the world?" In the first sentence of the section Jesus answers the question: "The answer to this question is-one." (M-12.1:1) I was somewhat confused by this chapter but Ken really clarified it for me. Ken tells us that Jesus is not talking about himself. When I study the *Course*, he's referring to me and when you study it for yourself, he's referring to you. The 2 pages of this Chapter 12 are much more understandable with this insight from Ken.

6. Ken tells us that: "If you do the *Course*, only do the *Course*." Those who decide they are going to mix the *Course* and, say Hinduism, may find many parallels but they'll also find differences and they'll likely get very confused. Early on in my study of the *Course*, when I realized that the material came from Jesus, it made sense to me that I wouldn't waste my time on anything else until I'd mastered the *Course*. Today, I look on this somewhat differently but coming to the same conclusion. If I fully master the *Course*, it means my mind is virtually always linked with Jesus and therefore with the Holy Spirit and Christ and I would have no need to study any other spirituality whatsoever – I'm on my way Home to Heaven.

7. Ken pointed out that Jesus tells us it's impossible to understand oneness (i.e., Heaven). "Truth [another word for Heaven or oneness] can only be experienced. It cannot be described and it cannot be explained." (T-8.VI.9:8-9)

Ken also points us to Lesson 169: "Oneness is simply the idea God is. And in His Being, He encompasses all things. No mind holds anything but Him. We say 'God is,' and then we cease to speak, for in that knowledge words are meaningless. There are no lips to speak them, and no part of mind sufficiently distinct to feel that it is now aware of something not itself. It has united with its Source [God]. And like its Source Itself, it merely is." (W-169.5:1-7)

I'm also including paragraph 10 from this lesson: "There is no need to further clarify what no one in the world can understand. When revelation of your oneness comes, it will be known and fully understood. [Authors note: This revelation has not yet happened for me but I've been moving towards it]. Now we [Jesus and I together] have work to do, for those in time [including me] can speak of things beyond, and listen to words which explain what is to come is past already. Yet what meaning can the words convey to those who count the hours still, and rise and work and go to sleep by them?" (W-169.10:1-4)

8. Often, Jesus makes reference in the *Course* to the communication between our Father and His Son in Heaven. Ken points out in the

workshop that the communication in Heaven has a totally different meaning than how the world defines it. In this world we usually think of this word as meaning someone communicating verbally or in writing to one or more other people. In Heaven, however, there is only one Mind and only glorious oneness. There is no consciousness in Heaven because this requires one entity to be conscious of another. The best I can come up with is Heaven's communication can be thought of as the ever extending Love which comes from God, and His Son and the Holy Spirit, Who are one with each other.

9. Ken reviews the three parts of our mind which are really quite simple:

> First, we have our spirit mind or God mind which is linked to the Holy Spirit (and Jesus and Christ) and ultimately causes us to return home to Heaven. It is perfectly sane.

> Second, we have our ego mind which tells us this world is real, we have sinned, God's going to punish the hell out of us, etc. It is perfectly insane.

> Third, there is a part of our mind here in this world that is *really* important although Jesus never specifically defines it. Jesus, however, makes reference to it many times. Ken defines it as the "decision maker" part of our mind. Lesson 155 provides a good example: "I will step back and let Him lead the way." My "decision maker" part of my mind has only 2 choices – to be guided by the ego's voice or to be guided by the Voice for God. What this Lesson 155 says is that my decision is to be guided by the Voice for God. I'll add to this that if this lesson were accomplished 100% by someone so that no ego thoughts are being considered then that individual has peaked in this world and has attained "real world" status as that term is defined in the *Course*.

10. Ken, in this workshop, reviews the initial separation idea which appears to have split us off from Heaven and the other splits which have brought us to the world we currently believe we're in today.

[I must, if I'm to progress in the *Course*, realize and experience better than I do now that Jimmy Laws is a dream figure that I made up, just as everything else in this world is part of <u>my</u> dream. I am literally not Jimmy Laws. I am Christ (God's only Son) just as you are.]

Before reviewing these different splits, following are two important paragraphs from the *Course* where Jesus describes the "tiny, mad idea" which crept into Heaven and was the basis for the first split:

"How willing are you to escape effects of all the dreams the world has ever had? Is it your wish to let no dream appear to be the cause of what it is you do? Then let us merely look upon the dream's beginning, for the part you see is but the second part, whose cause lies in the first. No one asleep and dreaming in the world remembers his attack upon himself. No one believes there really was a time when he knew nothing of a body, and could never have conceived this world as real. He would have seen at once that these ideas are one illusion, too ridiculous for anything but to be laughed away. How serious they now appear to be! And no one can remember when they would have met with laughter and disbelief. We can remember this if we look directly at their cause. And we will see the grounds for laughter, not a cause for fear." (T-27.VIII.5:1-10)

"Let us return the dream he gave away unto the dreamer, who perceives the dream as separate from himself and done to him. [Just imagine you, God's Son, and God are back in eternal Heaven before this physical world was made.] Into eternity, where all is one, there crept a tiny, mad idea, at which the Son of God remembered not to laugh. In his forgetting [to laugh] did the thought become a serious idea, and possible of both accomplishment and real effects. Together, we [Jesus and I] can laugh them both away, and understand that time cannot intrude upon eternity. It is a joke to think that time can come to circumvent eternity, which *means* there is no time." [In other words, just as the entire physical world is an illusion, time also is just an illusion.] (T-27.VIII.6:1-5)

Ken points out that when the "tiny, mad idea" crept into Heaven, there was only one Son Who obviously had a decision maker. When God's one Son decided to "run" with this idea and forgot to laugh was when the first split occurred and "all hell" appeared to start. The "tiny, mad idea" was, of course, from the ego.

Ken also pointed out that when we split, we forgot where we came from. So when the Son (appeared to have) separated from His Father at the first split, He forgot all about Heaven. He, of course, also forgot about God.

What Ken says is that at this point the Son has intolerable feelings of sin and guilt. The ego's answer to this is to make up a "God" who the Son can blame thereby alleviating or perhaps even eliminating His own sense of sin and guilt; it's "God's" fault, not mine. [Please note that when I refer to the ego's God I put quotes around the word God.]

At this point there's still no physical world although there is an ego "God" who is the victimizer and the separated Son (still just one) who is the poor victim. The separated Son realizes the odds against Him (it's Him against "God") and His fear is overwhelming. He needs a place to hide.

So the ego makes this physical world and also makes a body for the separated Son. Now the frightened Son has a place to hide but this apparently is not enough - the Son is still too frightened so the ego makes up other people so now the split off sons can blame each other as well as their victimizing and punishing "God."

Today, the number of split off sons is approximately 7.5 billion people.

This paragraph and the next few were not fully discussed in Ken's workshop but his workshop gave me the insights I have made. The story of Adam and Eve from the Bible is a perfect example of the ego's punishing "God" and man's blaming this "God" and his beautiful bride for the man's so-called sin. Here's how Adam was made by "God" according to the Bible: "- the Lord God formed the man from the dust of the ground and breathed into his nostrils the breath of life, and the man became a living being." (Genesis 2:7)

Then "God" made Eve: "So the Lord God caused the man to fall into a deep sleep; and while he was sleeping, he took one of the man's ribs and closed up the place with flesh. Then the Lord God made a woman from the rib he had taken out of the man, and he brought her to the man." (Genesis 2:21-22) Sometime after this, a talking serpent convinced Eve she should eat the fruit from the one tree in the garden which "God" had declared off limits. So Eve ate the forbidden fruit and gave some to Adam who was right there with her. Later on they of course got "caught" by "God" for their disobedience. Adam's response to "God" when asked if he had eaten the forbidden fruit is classic. In a simple sentence Adam blames both God and Eve for his disobedience: "The man said 'The woman you put here with me – she gave me some fruit from the tree, and I ate it.'" (Genesis 3:12) The way I interpret Adam's response is: "It's really not my fault. You, 'God', made the woman and she gave me the fruit." "God's" punishment for Adam and Eve was horrendous. He was obviously really "pissed off." His banishing them from the Garden of Eden was minor compared to their other consequences. If you want to you can read Genesis 3:16-24 to see what these were.

Let's go back to *A Course in Miracles* again and consider the initial separation splits that caused this illusionary world. The first ego thought was the "tiny, mad idea" that crept into Heaven. I think of this idea as "I, God's Son, will leave my Father and go off on my own." So God's one Son chose this idea, immediately forgot everything about Heaven and had overwhelming feelings of guilt and sin so the ego made up a "God" who the separated Son could blame. However, this led to traumatic fear because this "God" was a punishing God. All this happened "at once" so that even before the ego made the physical world, the one separated Son was full of sin, guilt and fear. The point I want to make here is that from the beginning of time, "Fear of God (i.e., the ego's 'God')" was something we have held on to. In his *Course*, Jesus tells us that we have to retrace our steps in order to wake up in Heaven. I think this is why, in the Section "The Obstacles to Peace" (T-19.IV), the last obstacle is the "The Fear of God." In other words, since the fear of "God" was right at the beginning in establishing our illusionary world, as we retrace our steps, it will be at the very end of our spiritual journey back home to Heaven. Following is a paragraph from the "Fear of God" sub-section of the *Course*:

> "Together we [Jesus and I] will disappear into the Presence beyond the veil, not to be lost but found; not to be seen but known. And knowing, nothing in the plan God has established for salvation will be left undone. This is the journey's purpose, without which is the journey meaningless. Here is the peace of God, given to you eternally by Him. Here is the rest and quiet that you seek, the reason for the journey from its beginning. Heaven is the gift you owe your brother [especially for me, my past special hate relationship I've had with Arkansas Ron], the debt of gratitude you offer to the Son of God in thanks for what he is, and what his Father created him to be." (T-19.IV.D.19:1-6)

In Section I of Chapter 2 of the *Course* (entitled "The Origins of Separation") Jesus uses the story of Adam as an analogy to tell us that this whole world can be thought of as a dream from God's one and only Son. Following are a few sentences from this Section:

> "The Garden of Eden, or the pre-separation condition [i.e., Heaven], was a state of mind in which nothing was needed. When Adam listened to the 'lies of the serpent' [i.e., the ego], all he heard was untruth." (T-2.I.3:1-2)

> "Yet the Bible says that a deep sleep fell upon Adam, and nowhere is there reference to his waking up. The world has not yet experienced any comprehensive reawakening or rebirth." (T-2.I.3:6-7)

> "Only after the deep sleep fell upon Adam could he experience nightmares." (T-2.I.4:5)

Using *A Course in Miracles* terminology, God and His one and only Son (Adam) were in Heaven (the Garden of Eden) and His Son listened to some "tiny, mad idea" (the first lie from the serpent) and God's Son (Adam) fell into a coma (a deep sleep). The entire history of the world is simply the nightmare of God's only Son (Adam). About 2,000 years ago, the first individual within the total nightmare woke up and his name, of course, is Jesus. Since then, there have been a few others who have awakened (as I understand spiritual history) but not a whole lot. As Jesus says in his *Course*, there has not yet been any comprehensive reawakening or rebirth.

11. Ken helped me appreciate that there are only 2 thought systems here on earth. One is the ego's which is all illusion and continuously separates and the other is God's which is all Truth and continuously unites. True happiness can only be obtained from God's thought system.

12. Ken pointed out that everyone on earth has the same purpose which is to remember who we are which is God's one and only Son so we can wake up in Heaven. I'll add that, although we left (or fell asleep) as God's one Son, it's noteworthy that we wake up individually. Jesus was the first of the separated sons to wake up which is why he is the model and teacher we try to mentally join with. He is also my best friend because he, not I, knows what's best for me.

13. Ken spent quite a bit of time talking about Jesus telling us that we want to be "above the battleground." This discussion by Ken, in my recent listening of this workshop, helped me learn more about Jesus' *Course* teachings than any other part of the workshop so thank you yet once again Ken.

One of the things Ken said was that Jesus wants us to literally join with him in our minds when we go "above the battleground" and think "outside the world" (or "outside the box" if we use the worldly cliché). Since Jesus is 100% joined with Christ, I too become 100% joined with Christ when I fully join with Jesus. And, of course, Christ is our God given Reality.

From this reference point, "above the battleground" with Jesus, I can see that this entire world is truly just <u>my</u> dream. I made up my lovely wife Tesha and our two wonderful children and our spunky dog, Ollie. I made up the sun, the stars, the snow, the rain, the cities, the history of my world as I see it, etc. I also made up Arkansas Ron who appears not to like me. I made up Donald Trump, Dolly Parton, Ken Wapnick, etc.

What I didn't understand, and this was my greatest epiphany from this most recent listening to this workshop from Ken, was that I made up me, Jimmy Laws. However, as I now think of it, the simple reason is extremely obvious. I have said many times and for many years that each of us is, in truth, Christ, God's one Son. Clearly, I can't be both Jimmy Laws and Christ. The truth is I'm Christ and Jimmy Laws is just an illusionary person who is part of my dream just as is everything else in this world.

In Section 23.IV (entitled "Above the Battleground") of his *Course*, Jesus spends about two pages discussing what this idea means. Paragraph 8, as I understand it, tells us what it is like once all ego thoughts have no interest for us and we only listen to the Voice for God, just as Jesus was able to do:

> "Think what is given those who share their Father's purpose, and who know that it is theirs. They want for nothing. Sorrow of any kind is inconceivable. Only the light they love is in awareness, and only love shines upon them forever. It is their past, their present and their future; always the same, eternally complete and wholly shared. They know it is impossible their happiness could ever suffer change of any kind. Perhaps you think the battleground [i.e., the world] can offer something you can win. Can it be something that offers you a perfect calmness, and a sense of love so deep and quiet that no touch of doubt can ever mar your certainty? And that will last forever?" (T-23.IV.8:1-9)

Ken pointed out that when we're in the "real world", we <u>always</u> know this world is a dream. This is why Jesus never suffered when his body was nailed to the cross – he knew nothing happened.

Ken referred us to the following *Course* sentences: "The miracle establishes you dream a dream, and that its content is not true. [Most important for me is to remember Jimmy Laws is just some fictional character I made up.] This is a crucial step in dealing with illusions." (T-28.II.7:1-2)

Ken pointed out that when we stay fully aware it's a dream "all the time", we won't react at all.

When we literally join with Jesus in our minds, we join with oneness.

14. Here are some other notes I took while listening to Ken's workshop:

A Course in Miracles teaches us how to listen to Jesus so we can unlearn all the ego's blocks to truth (a synonym for Heaven). Give Jesus a chance to be my <u>only teacher.</u> When I (or the ego) was my teacher, it brought progressive unhappiness leading to death. With Jesus as my – ever increasing – teacher, it's brought progressive happiness leading to everlasting life.

Healing is about healing my relationship with Myself Who is Christ.

Forget about joining with anyone out there because there's no one out there! It's all my dream! On the other hand, I can tell you I have made a tremendous number of friends in the world since I started studying the *Course.* Fear of people has essentially disappeared from my mindset. Somewhere in the *Course,* Jesus talks of this phenomenon where everyone in the world becomes our friend. However, a very important set of truths mentioned a lot by Jesus in the *Course* underlies Ken's point here. One very important point is the reminder of where we all came from – Heaven – where there is but one all encompassing Mind (God plus His Creation) and there is literally no separation whatsoever (i.e., the idea of "joining" physically is ludicrous). Another important point that Jesus mentions is that the purpose of the *Course* is to allow us to remove the barriers which are blocking us from being in Heaven using his help and the help of the Holy Spirit and Christ. As these barriers are removed, we become extremely loveable people and we do have many friends and, while doing so, we understand on an increasing basis, that these people are really illusions we made up in our minds, as Ken pointed out.

The *Course* is simple. Jesus tells us this in the *Course* and he also tells us that he's done his best to explain things so that students won't misinterpret his teachings. My own personal experience is that both of these our true – it's simple and understandable. However, it takes a lot of dedicated self-study time to benefit from the *Course*. Further, the gift of the *Course* for me is the more I study it, the more understandable it becomes to me and the happier I become.

Everyone in this world has major control issues. A simple example is: "If only she would do what I want her to do then I would be happy." So now this person tries to persuade her (i.e., control her) in order to be happy. One thing I've learned from the *Course* is happiness is 100% an inside job and the logical reason is that everything that appears outside of me is really coming from within me. It's all my dream!

The "thirst for knowledge" as the world defines it is opposite of the "thirst for Knowledge (or truth or God)" just as the entire world is opposite of the "Oneness of God." This brings to mind the word "power". The United States is the most "powerful" country in the world because of our arsenal of weapons and troops. The "power" of God clearly has nothing to do with this destructive meaning. On the contrary, we are in a place of eternal peace when we have God's power. Note that the ego's "God", on the other hand, is often considered to be very punishing and destructive.

Once the world is real, it's not easy to get out of it. In his *Course*, Jesus points out that to everyone who ever came here, there was no question that the world was real. Clearly, this includes Jesus himself when he was a young man. At one point in the *Course*, Jesus effectively says if I, Jesus, can "wake up" (as he clearly did) then so can we. Ken also pointed out that to make a better dream (i.e., a better world) has nothing to do with the *Course*.

I'm not the victim of anything out there. I'm only a victim of my dream. In other words, I'm only the victim of me.

I should question everything I think or ever thought was meaningful. This is consistent with Lesson 128 – "The world I see holds nothing that I want." What helps me easily keep my perspective in this regard is where Jesus tells us that our "loving thoughts" do stay with us when we journey on (i.e., when we "die").

We are all "one." I'll use my lovely wife, Tesha, in this example. It is true that Tesha and I are one. However, the joining of Tesha and I physically is not my purpose and has nothing to do with us "being one". I am "one" with everybody and everything in this world. What Ken effectively said and, of course, Jesus says is: "Remember, Jimmy, you made Tesha up."

Ken talked about being scared in the world for any reason such as when it appears a runaway truck is about to slam into my car or an apparent thief is following me home. During any such fear episodes, Ken says I've effectively told God I'm right because it wasn't my fault …. so He's wrong. This simply shows that I still believe I'm a body and that this world is real. I did in fact make up this fear because I have made up this entire world. It's all my dream!

An illusion is an illusion is….etc. All illusions are –o-. There is no world! When I judge others, I forget this.

This is okay *Course* thinking: "I still believe I'm in the world but I know my belief is a dream which never happened and from which I will wake up."

All fear is within me because the ego is within me.

Act appropriately in the world. Everything in this world is a symbol of darkness. However, with the help of Jesus (and the Holy Spirit and Christ) these all get turned into symbols of light and using vision we see the light of Heaven on the other side of all symbols. As this occurs, the world becomes a beautiful place.

Get back to the gate of Heaven in a Holy Instant. My current verbal shortened Holy Instant, which I use many times every day, is: "I'm sane and serene forever and ever and ever. Above the battleground, I am determined to join with you, Jesus. Thus, I am Christ, the same as you. Jesus tells me: 'Let's go straight to the gate of Heaven and look both ways.' I first look at Heaven and see only eternal peace. [Now I'm in a 'Holy Instant.'] Then, without using my eyes, I look at the world knowing it's all illusion especially the body and life of Jimmy Laws [I accept Atonement for myself]."

Although I have learned a lot over the past 18 years, I had not really learned that "Jimmy Laws (i.e., me)" was simply a part of my own dream. As a direct result of this third time listening to this workshop, when I go above the battleground, I join with Jesus and I think "This person sitting here (or standing or lying here) is not who I am." As Jesus tells us many times in his *Course*, I am the same as he is and we are Christ, God's only Son. And whoever might be reading this, you are Christ also. This idea, of course, must be taken literally.

We are not asked to give up the world and its things but to perceive them differently, with our right mind listening to the Holy Spirit (or Jesus or Christ) and not with our wrong mind listening to the ego.

The *Course* must work if I do what it says and it's 100% up to me: The problem (the ego) is within me and the solution (God's Voice) is within me. Many people agree that happiness is totally (100%) an inside job. What this idea tells us is that misery or unhappiness is also totally (100%) an inside job.

There is one name: GOD!

Forgiveness – The undoing of everything the ego had done.

Important to me – We join with Jesus. This is the ultimate joining because when my mind is joined with my best friend, Jesus, it must also be joined with the Holy Spirit, with Christ and with God Himself. I'm right at the gate of Heaven.

An idea from the *Course* is that when you find yourself in a desert the best thing you can do is to leave the desert. The analogy, as Ken pointed out, is that the ego thought system is a desert and we should therefore leave it behind us.

Jesus, as we know, was just a young man when he was crucified. Ken pointed out, however, that today he's about 2,000 years wiser than he was then.

We are all insane and Jesus tells us this numerous times in his *Course*. Naturally, we shouldn't take this personally. If we weren't insane at some level, we wouldn't be able to stay here on earth for very long.

Forgiveness is not love. Love is impossible in this world. Forgiveness itself is an illusion (which is understandable to me because clearly in Heaven forgiveness is not necessary at all). However, forgiveness is the essential illusion we must learn here because it is the <u>only</u> illusion that leads towards love.

Nothing outside of me is the cause of my unhappiness.

The happy dream is a <u>process</u> whereby we become aware that we are not who we thought we were. For example, I am not Jimmy Laws; I am Christ, the same as you.

The following are literal statements: "I am not here at all." "It's all been my dream."

This is a "nondualistic" course to the core. Another word for nondualistic is oneness so we can say: This is a "oneness" course to the core.

When we choose right mindedness "only" (i.e., when we adhere only to the Voice for God and never to the ego's voice) we attain the "real world" and slip into Heaven.

I made up the idea that Jesus was crucified on the cross (in my dream). I'm quite sure you did the same thing in your dream.

Chapter 12 of the Manual for Teachers asks the question: "How many teachers of God are needed to save the world?" The first sentence of the section gives us the answer: "The answer to this question is – one." Ken points out that I am that one. This is not at all egocentric when I put it all together for me: This entire world is a dream that I made up and what I need do is to forgive my world; to forgive the world is to see that this world is but my dream and not real so there is nothing to forgive.

Important note: Many times in the *Course* Jesus points out that God only has one Son, who he also defines as Christ. We are, in truth, all that one Son. Jesus is Christ, you are Christ, I am Christ and all other people in the world are also Christ. The last sentence in the preceding paragraph is easily understood by me when I think of me as God's one Son or Christ (and not as Jimmy Laws). Given this, I can re-write the last sentence as follows:

> This is not at all egocentric when I put it all together for Me (Christ): This entire world is a dream that I made up (which began when I chose the "tiny, mad idea and forgot to laugh") and what I need do is to forgive My world; to forgive the world is to see that this world is but My dream and not real so there is nothing to forgive.

Part III - me

Chapter 1: My family life growing up

I was born in Brooklyn on October 19, 1949. When I was only 2 years old, our family moved to North Bellmore, Long Island, New York.

I was the second oldest of 5 children and, when I look back today, I had an ideal upbringing. We were a family of 7 people who really worked as a team.

We were not wealthy yet all our needs were met so we really lacked for nothing. My Dad sold Fuller Brush door to door and the income from that job paid our bills. When my youngest sister started going to school, my Mom started working as a waitress in a family restaurant. I was about 15 at the time.

One thing we looked forward to every year was our family vacation. We always took 2 weeks every summer and headed up to Rogers Rock Campground on the shores of Lake George in upstate New York. Our "house" for those 2 weeks was a large heavy canvas tent that my Dad set up for us. I have wonderful memories of those vacations.

During all my growing up years we ate supper every night as a family except on Sundays, which was my Dad's day off. On Sunday we had a deluxe dinner in the mid-afternoon which might have been a roast beef or ham or meat loaf with baked or mashed potatoes with gravy and, of course, a couple of vegetables.

One strict rule my Dad had was that we better be around when it came time for the family meal. I don't ever remember breaking this rule though I probably did from time to time.

My father had another strict rule which I didn't like at all. From a very young age, all 5 of us kids were required to go to Sunday school and church every Sunday until we were confirmed at about age 13. We went to our local Lutheran church. The reason I didn't like it was that I felt I had to go to school 5 days a week and Saturdays and Sundays should be exclusively for me to play and have fun. Church obligations and social activities were never fun for me. Many years later, when I was in my 50's, I understood that my Dad felt it was part of his parental responsibility to see that his children had some religious education. So he was just being a responsible parent.

So I went to church religiously until I was about 13 years old. I recall the last 2 years, just before confirmation, were the worst because we were required to go to confirmation class on Saturday as well as Sunday school and worship service on Sunday. Talk about messing up 'my' weekends! I don't ever remember making any friends at these religious activities nor learning anything about God or the Bible. For a long time I held the belief that Jesus was a mythical figure just as I had of course learned Santa Claus was. The only thing I liked about Sunday school and confirmation class is that, unlike regular school, I didn't have to learn anything to advance from one grade to the next.

Up until age 15, when we moved to a new house in a different neighborhood and school district, my best and really only friend was Tommy, who lived directly across the street from us. Tommy and I were inseparable when we weren't in school or had family obligations. We went fishing, hiking, built forts, captured a wild possum once, took bike hikes over some long distances, and many other things including some malicious pranks for which we seldom got caught.

As a rule, I was a lazy student. I only did homework if I really had to and usually at the last minute. However, with respect to math, I was really gifted. With virtually no effort, I understood my math teachers when they taught us from the blackboard in class and, when I did the assigned homework, it was more like solving easy puzzles and really wasn't "work" at all. I think I always got A's in my math classes from my earliest memories right through the end of high school.

Because of my math aptitude, I had a major turning point in 11th grade. A man representing *The College of Insurance* (located in Manhattan) came to our math class and talked to us about the actuarial profession. Basically what I heard him say was that an actuary was someone who passed 10 exams and became a highly paid executive in the insurance industry. To pass these exams, a person had to be very proficient in mathematics. Being absolutely convinced at the time that money and happiness were absolutely linked (the more money I had, the happier I would be) combined with my ability to easily pass math exams, I had decided on my career path that day.

Chapter 2: My move to New York City for college and career

In the fall of 1967, just shy of my 18th birthday, I moved into New York City with a friend of mine from high school who was also going to The College of Insurance (TCI). We rented an apartment on West 10th Street in Manhattan, just a short distance from the Hudson River. TCI was of the work-study kind where the student gets a sponsoring employer which pays two thirds of the student's tuition and employs the student every other semester. My sponsoring employer was New York Life Insurance Company (NYL). So here's how it worked for me: from September through December of 1967, I completed my 1st semester of school at TCI; from January through April of 1968, I worked at NYL; from May through August of 1968, I was back at TCI for my second semester of school; etc. It took about 5 years to complete all 8 semesters of school.

A major family tragedy occurred in December of 1967. My Mom passed away as a result of a car accident. Although it tore up my Dad emotionally, I was already on my own path and not living at home so I was not a firsthand witness to how much my Dad was hurting. I do know that my two oldest sisters – Ellie who's a year older than me and Cindy who's about a year and a half younger than me – supported him and our two younger siblings at great levels. At the time I was much too selfish to be of any help even if I had been living at home. With the hindsight I have gained since then, I often thank God for the strength these two sisters of mine had during that tumultuous time.

What I did not know about the Bible truly came to light when I was about 20 and in college. In a literature class, the professor assigned us the "Book of Job" from the Old Testament as a reading assignment. I was truly surprised because, for the first time in my life, I realized that the Bible actually consisted of stories. Prior to that, I somehow thought the Bible was just a bunch of little thoughts with no continuity from one sentence to the next. So you can see, as I still can, that all those hours in religious training in my young years were largely wasted on me.

The years I was employed at New York Life were good ones. I worked in the pension department and learned a lot about this aspect of the insurance business. The social aspect there was also very good. I got to meet a lot of people and established many good friendships within the Company. By the time I left New York Life in 1976, I had passed 6 of the 10 actuarial exams.

One of the persons I got to know was a pretty and perky young lady named Debbie. Debbie also worked in the pension department but in a different section than I did. Periodically, Debbie required some technical input from the actuarial section where I worked and would come to me for answers. I got the feeling she liked me and in late 1974 I built up all my courage and asked Debbie for her phone number which she gave me. We started dating and by early 1975 we were engaged to be married. In early 1976, I was offered a very promising job working for a national employee benefits consulting firm (The Segal Company) in their Los Angeles office which I accepted. So in the spring of 1976, Debbie and I had a very nice wedding in Brooklyn, New York with our family and friends and the next day we flew to Los Angeles (with Debbie's two cats) to start our new married life in California.

Chapter 3: My marriage to Debbie

Overall, our marriage was a good one. Although I had made very good progress in my career back in New York, an important part of my personal life included the use of mind altering illegal drugs and alcohol so naturally my friends I hung around with also did the same thing. This actually began when I was 15 years old. Within a year of our marriage, Debbie let me know that this type of activity would have to be curtailed. So during the 17 years of our marriage, my drug use virtually stopped and, unless we had a party at our home, I never drank any alcohol there.

By 1978, we had bought and moved into a small house in Eagle Rock, California, a small city near Pasadena. While we lived there, we were blessed with a little baby girl we named Kimberly (Today, Kim is a single lady doing very well and living up in Clinton, Massachusetts).

Two important events occurred in 1979. We bought and moved into a brand new 4-bedroom house in La Verne, California. Shortly after we moved in, I remember standing in the front yard and thinking "Wow! Now I've got everything I ever dreamed of – A pretty wife, a healthy little baby girl and a beautiful house. What else is there to strive for?" My spiritual thinking at the time can best be described as atheistic - life was in the here and now and when one died that was the end of everything. The answer I came up with was to strive for advancement in the Segal Company with a higher salary and more "stuff." Since I really enjoyed my work and my new employer, this was a very acceptable answer to my question.

The other important event that occurred in 1979 was that I passed the last actuarial exam and, having completed all 10 of the exams, I was now a "Fellow of the Society of Actuaries." So after about 12 years of very hard study, I had reached my professional goal. Perhaps even more important in my mind was that all that personal time which I'd been spending on my studies would now be available for more "fun times."

In October, 1980, Debbie gave birth to our son Derek. So now we were blessed with two beautiful healthy children and life was really good. (Today, Derek is a single man doing very well and living in Portsmouth, Virginia.)

I don't recall the exact year but I think it was around 1981 that I was diagnosed with bipolar chemical imbalance (at the time, this disease was referred to as manic depression but the medical profession has since changed its name to bipolar chemical imbalance). Approximately 1% of Americans have this disease. For all people, our brains rely on good electrical impulses in order for them to work properly. For those of us who have bipolar chemical imbalance, the electrical impulses aren't working properly because of a chemical imbalance in our brains but psychiatrists have found that certain medications solve or at least alleviate the problem. There is a significant amount of trial and error, however, because while certain medications will work for one person's bipolar brain, a different set of medications might be required for someone else's bipolar brain. I am pleased to report that I have been on the same two medications for many years and see my psychiatrist on a regular basis; this problem appears to be totally in check for me.

Although I'm doing very well in recent years with my brain's chemical balance, this bipolar disease raised its gory head on numerous occasions over the past 35 years. Suffice it to say that some of my worldly adventures and misadventures, described here in Part III, were at least partly attributable to this bipolar disease.

By around 1982, Debbie and I had purchased a pop-up tent trailer and used it every summer for about 10 consecutive years. While in California, we would leave for at least two weeks and spend typically two or three nights in any one campground before moving on to the next one. This allowed us to visit quite a few different areas in the Western United States each summer. We all loved it and looked forward to it every summer. It also instilled the joy of camping and swimming and hiking and traveling, etc., in both Kim and Derek.

In 1986, I was given the opportunity to become the manager of the actuarial department in Segal Company's Boston office. After discussing this with Debbie, we decided it was a good idea. One of the primary factors was that we were quite close to Debbie's mother (Dovie) and her step-father (Joe) who lived in Brooklyn, New York and Boston was only about a 4 hour drive to their home. So by the Fall of 1986, we had made the big move and were living in a large home in Wayland, Massachusetts, a very nice suburban town due west of Boston. Our summer vacations from 1987 until 1992 consisted of visiting much of the Northeastern and Mid-Atlantic portions of the United States in our old reliable pop-up tent trailer.

By the early 1990's I had been named a Senior Vice President of the Segal Company. My responsibilities included managing the actuarial department in our Boston Office (supervising approximately 7 other professionals) as well as having consulting responsibilities to some of our major client pension funds. My consulting duties required me to attend pension board meetings in different cities around the country on a regular basis. Typically, I was gone for 2 or 3 nights when I attended such meetings. I enjoyed all aspects of my job.

I was doing okay until mid-1993 when I separated from Debbie and the family home. Here's what happened. For Christmas of 1992, I purchased a $600 camcorder for the family. I knew it would be a great gift because it would allow us to capture, in movie form, the memorable family activities, including birthdays, holidays and especially our wonderful summer vacations. Well, when Debbie opened this gift that Christmas, she was really upset. We seldom communicated our feelings but I believe her thinking was "How could you (meaning me) spend this kind of money without first talking to me!" I know my thinking was "Over this entire marriage, I have been the sole bread winner and have always made sure our bills are paid so what right do you have to question me!" It's possible we yelled these fixed ideas back and forth at each other but I don't recall. This incident, however, was the proverbial "straw that broke the camel's back" and, after mulling it over in my mind for perhaps a couple of weeks, I informed Debbie that I would be divorcing her. So the extreme tension between Debbie and I that began on Christmas continued for about 6 months when I moved out of the family house.

Chapter 4: Separation and divorce from Debbie

Beginning with that very first day I was out of the family home, I could see that "I was free at last" yet felt very angry at the same time. That night, I ended up staying at an upscale motel with a lively bar and good music and I happily drank myself into oblivion. I no longer had to be concerned with "not drinking" at home.

Meanwhile, on that same day, Debbie had a restraining order taken out against me so I was not allowed on the premises of my own house. I was blocked off from everything I had worked so hard to acquire. Hence, the tremendous anger that I was feeling.

Although some divorces are accomplished on a mature and friendly basis, ours was to be the more common nasty type.

The next 4 years are somewhat of a blur for me because of ongoing drugging and drinking wherever possible. It was on August 15, 1997, that I had my last drug or drink which is when my new spiritual life started to unfold. In the paragraphs which follow are some of the highlights that I remember from mid-1993 until August of 1997 as I slid ever deeper into the hell of addiction.

After I separated from Debbie in mid-1993, I rented an apartment in Marlboro, Massachusetts which is only two towns from Wayland where the family home was located. In 1994, I moved from the rented apartment into a condominium which I purchased, also in Marlboro.

In addition to my new habit of doing drugs and drinking excessive amounts of alcohol, I immediately started another habit which on the surface would appear positive. I began studying the Bible and attending church regularly. My study of the Bible was obsessive. I studied it every night; I studied it when I commuted on the train into work; and I studied it during my lunch break at work. I was clearly looking for God although I was, at the same time, becoming ever more insane as my addictions became progressively worse. With the hindsight I have today, I can tell you (with a smile) that a doped up drunken Bible thumping individual is not attractive to anyone else in the world.

My job performance, of course, was adversely impacted. I had been an exceptional employee for 17 years. Also, my employer was very aware of my bipolar disease. The thinking of my office manager and other senior executives of the Segal Company was that the stress of the divorce combined with the death of my father, also in 1993, were the cause of my dysfunction on the job. Their hope was that my deterioration was a temporary condition which I would recover from.

An incident occurred at the end of 1993 which caused me to stop drinking and drugging on my own. To the best of my recollection, I'd been drinking heavily every night at my apartment for about 6 months. Shortly before Christmas, we were having our office Christmas party and my plan was to be real careful with my drinking. I recall thinking that I would just drink lightly and only white wine. I probably started out with a glass of white wine but I ended up in a blackout drunk because I have no recall of that evening until I woke up in my plush office which overlooked Copley Square in Boston – it was about 3 in the morning. Apparently, I at least had enough sense to realize I was too drunk to drive home and made my way to my office to "sleep it off." My car was parked in the parking lot underneath our office building. When I woke up at 3 in the morning, I felt sober enough to drive home to my apartment in Marlboro. The drive consisted of about 25 minutes on the Massachusetts Turnpike and then about 15 minutes of dimly lit winding roads through the little towns of the Boston suburbs. I remember feeling quite comfortable driving home. However, when I reached home and went to put the lights off in my Dodge Caravan, I realized I had never put them on and this really shook me up – I was so lucky not to have been stopped by the police and put in jail for driving under the influence of alcohol with whatever costs and other consequences might be involved. This "fear" episode caused me to not drink or drug for the next 12 months. So for virtually all of 1994, I remained clean and sober.

Chapter 5: My rebound marriage to Lucy

In the spring of 1994, I was legally divorced from Debbie. Around that time I started dating a cute Brazilian lady named Lucy who I had met in church. In October of 1994 Lucy and I were married, convinced that this was a marriage "made in Heaven." Well, it didn't take long to realize that it wasn't. My home life, both before and after Lucy moved in, consisted of me obsessively studying the Bible. I do recall Lucy pointing out to me that she would like me to spend a little time with her such as watching some TV together. However, it never crossed my mind at the time that she might have a valid point; my study of the Bible was clearly more important than watching anything on television.

Lucy and I had a major yelling argument sometime in December. About two weeks after this, I came home from work to find Lucy and all her stuff were gone. Sometimes when I share this history with someone, I tell them "Lucy was a lot smarter than Debbie because she only stayed with me for 2 months whereas Debbie was with me for 17 years." (smile)

Lucy's departure occurred just before Christmas of 1994 and I had done no drugging or drinking for the past 12 months. I don't recall exactly when – it might have been the same day that Lucy left – but in a very short time I was back to drugging and drinking "like a fish" once again and I wouldn't stop until I hit "rock bottom" in August of 1997.

Chapter 6: Single once again

At least for the next year (1995), I held on to the fear of getting a dui (drinking under the influence of alcohol) and made a point not to be driving when I was drinking. There was a nice bar about 1-1/2 miles from my condo which I enjoyed. To avoid any dui possibility, I always walked to this bar which had 2 or 3 pool tables. Since I really enjoyed drinking and playing pool, I frequented this establishment on a regular basis and I could get good and drunk since I didn't have to drive home.

On my walk to this bar (which was along Route 20 for those familiar with the western suburbs of Boston) I passed a liquor store. This store was generally open as I was walking to "my" bar and I knew it would be closed when I was walking back home so I'd stop in on the way to the bar and purchase vodka, rum, tequila or whatever my heart desired for my home consumption. Never considering (until this writing) that I probably could have asked the bartender at the bar to hold this booze for me until I left the bar, what I did was to hide my booze in a patch of trees somewhere along Route 20 as I continued walking to my bar and would pick it up on my walk home. The problem was that by the time I left the bar I was so inebriated it was sometimes really difficult to find my booze. I have some recollection of one night spending a lot of time looking frantically for my hidden booze and, finally finding it, I had such relief and joy, I internally cried out "Thank you God! You're wonderful." When Jesus said "Seek and ye shall find", I don't think he was referring to this type of episode but it sure worked for me that night! (smile)

For the rest of 1995, my so-called social life largely consisted of drinking at my home bar as described above or drinking at home. When I was at the office, I was seldom drunk but my performance level had deteriorated significantly. Around the middle of 1995, I was no longer supervising the actuarial department, all or virtually all of my consulting clients were given to other senior employees and I was given entry level duties. My employer kept paying me my $100,000 salary with the hope that I would soon return to the valuable employee I had been for so many years.

Chapter 7: My employer gives up hope and fires me

Sometime in the fall of 1995, I found myself in a mental hospital right in my new hometown of Marlboro, Massachusetts. After being there for perhaps a couple of weeks, I had a visit from my office manager from the Boston office and an executive vice president from the Chicago office of the company. They informed me that I was fired but that my salary would be continued for 8 months.

Shortly after this, I was released from the hospital and felt freedom like I had probably never felt it before. Not only did I no longer have any real family obligations but now I was free of any obligations to an employer. I should mention, if you haven't figured it out yet, that I was totally out of my mind but I didn't have a clue.

I decided to visit some old friends in the Oklahoma City area and then head on to California to spend Christmas with my step sister, Helen, and her children and so I did. Despite a lot of drinking and drugging during this trip, I somehow made it back to my condo in Massachusetts without any lockups in jails or insane asylums. Although 1996 is a big blur, I think I arrived back home around February or March of 1996.

While I was in Oklahoma, I fell madly in love with a single mom and her two young children. We stayed in touch by phone. This obsessive infatuation with this very nice lady resulted in me deciding to pay her a surprise visit so, shortly after I was back home in Massachusetts, I hopped into my Dodge Caravan and headed back west to Oklahoma. When I reached her sister's house where she was staying and knocked on the door, she was happily surprised to see me and the two of us went out to dinner.

During dinner, I ended up getting drunk and embarrassed her in front of one of her college professors who happened to be dining at the same restaurant. She was livid! She was pissed! Though my efforts to win her back were insanely extreme, to the best of my recollection I have never seen her since that night.

I ended up staying in Oklahoma for a while. Around the middle of 1996, I got a dui in Norman, Oklahoma. This was to be the 1st of 11 lockups I was to have until I stopped drugging and drinking in August of 1997. Here's a brief summary of these as best I can remember them:

1. The 1st dui in Norman, Oklahoma mentioned above.
2. A 2nd dui also in Norman only 2 weeks after the first one.
3. Shortly after my 2nd dui, I drove to Buffalo, N.Y., where I have family members. My first day there, I attempted suicide by taking a whole bunch of depakote capsules (prescribed for my bipolar illness). I spent a week or so in a medical hospital followed by about 3 weeks in a Buffalo psychiatric hospital.
4. While visiting my son in Massachusetts, I got drunk and was arrested for public intoxication.
5. Sometime in the fall of 1996, while living in a flea bag motel in Buffalo, I wanted my friend and neighbor (he rented the motel room right next to mine) to join me for some drinking but he had to work the next day so he told me no. I kept harassing him and even threatened I would call the police and have him arrested for disturbing the peace if he didn't join me. This didn't work so, being a man of my word, I called the police on my neighbor. A short while later the police arrived and naturally I got taken off to jail for disturbing the peace. When drinking, I often made some very dumb decisions – smile.
6. Right after the breakup of me and a new girlfriend in Buffalo, I borrowed/stole her son's bicycle from her front porch. She reported this to my sister which led me to a 2 or 3 week stay in the psychiatric ward of the Erie County Medical Center in Buffalo.
7. At some point, I spent another stint in the psychiatric ward of the Erie County Medical Center but I don't recall what I had done to cause this.
8. Towards the end of 1996 or perhaps early 1997, I flew back to Oklahoma City for a little while. During this trip, at one point I argued with a cab driver: I angrily insisted that he play music from his radio and stop listening to the dispatcher. As I recall, this heated argument caused him to drop me off short of my destination with the understanding I wouldn't pay him for the aborted ride. However, he called the police and I got myself locked up once again in Oklahoma.
9. One night, while on this trip to Oklahoma, I came to the conclusion that the world was about to blow up and I must fly to Boston to save my two children, Kim and Derek. I was very much out of my mind

of course. So I packed my few belongings and took a cab to the airport. When I got to the right airline which had flights to Boston, I learned that all the computers were down and they couldn't sell any tickets. I then decided to return to the city and ended up getting into a heated argument with a car rental agent who wouldn't call a cab for me. She did, however, call the cops on me. This provided me with a very nice stay in the best mental hospital I've ever stayed in, somewhere in Norman, Oklahoma. As I recall, I stayed there about 6 weeks.

10. I was able to get back to Buffalo at some point after this. Shortly after my return to Buffalo, I interviewed at a local grocery store to be a cashier and the manager told me she would call me within a week or two. One day while drinking heavily in my apartment (I had moved up from the flea bag motel), I became real angry at this lady because she hadn't called me. So I called her up and, to the best of my recollection, she didn't apologize nor tell me whether or not I had the job. I was pissed! Having nothing better to do, I kept calling her back, harassing her and using some nasty language. I think I was probably still calling her when someone knocked on my apartment door – two policemen were there, put handcuffs on me and carried me off to jail. I smile at this a lot – There's not too many people who get locked up while drugging and drinking alone at home.

11. One time in Buffalo, I actually voluntarily checked myself into Brylin Hospital, a mental health facility. I was feeling that my whole body was about to blow up from the inside out. I had talked to my psychiatrist during the day on the phone and he told me that if I couldn't make it until the next morning when he could see me, then I could check myself into the hospital. Late that night, I took a cab to the hospital.

Here's an interesting note to my story. When I took that trip to Oklahoma in late 1996 or early 1997, I ran out of money because my credit card company had cut me off. At the time, my drinking buddy was a homeless man named Pops. On the day we ran out of money, we took a cab to the underneath of a bridge where Pops had stayed before (the cab fare represented the last of our funds). Another homeless man was also living there with his dog and, as far as I was concerned, it was great. We had booze, perhaps some food, a dog and a roof over our heads (the bridge above us). It was a new experience for me and I was truly happy. I was also quite drunk at the time.

So in a about a year, from late 1995 until late 1996 or early 1997, I went from an unhappy senior vice president of a consulting company with a $100,000 salary to a happy homeless guy with two friends and a dog and I was penniless.

Unfortunately, within a few hours a policeman came by and told us we could not stay under the bridge. The two friends and the dog ran off and I was alone. I ended up at a nearby 24-hour fast food restaurant, someone gave me change so I could call my sister in Buffalo and she wired me some money via Western Union so I could get back to Buffalo. A few days later, I was taking a bus back home to Buffalo.

I'm very pleased to tell you that since I stopped drugging and drinking in August of 1997, I have never been locked up in any jail or psychiatric hospital.

Chapter 8: A brief discussion of 12-step recovery programs

For me, I think of the 12-step program I belong to as an essential powerful undergraduate program in spirituality and *A Course in Miracles* as a most powerful mind training graduate program in spirituality. I have adopted both as a way of life. Note that neither program has anything to do with organized (i.e., formal) religion.

There are many dozens of different 12-step programs. To give you an idea, following are just a few in alphabetic order:

AA – Alcoholics Anonymous

Al-Anon – For friends and families of alcoholics

CoDA – Co-Dependents Anonymous

EA – Emotions Anonymous

GA – Gamblers Anonymous

NA – Narcotics Anonymous

OA – Overeaters Anonymous

SA – Sex Addicts Anonymous

WA – Workaholics Anonymous

Most 12-step programs follow the same formula that was established by the first 12-step program, Alcoholics Anonymous, which began in 1935. These 12 steps are as follows:

1. We admitted we were powerless over "whatever the addiction or problem" – that our lives had become unmanageable.
2. We came to believe that a power greater than ourselves could restore us to sanity.
3. We made a decision to turn our will and our lives over to the care of God as we understood Him.
4. We made a searching and fearless moral inventory of ourselves.

5. We admitted to God, to ourselves, and to another human being the exact nature of our wrongs.
6. We were entirely ready to have God remove all these defects of character.
7. We humbly asked Him to remove our shortcomings.
8. We made a list of all persons we had harmed, and became willing to make amends to them all.
9. We made direct amends to such people wherever possible, except when to do so would injure them or others.
10. We continued to take personal inventory and when we were wrong promptly admitted it.
11. We sought through prayer and meditation to improve our conscious contact with God as we understood Him, praying only for knowledge of His will for us and the power to carry that out.
12. Having had a spiritual awakening as the result of these steps, we tried to carry this message to "other persons with the same addiction or problem", and to practice these principles in all our affairs.

One significant parallel between these 12 step programs and *A Course in Miracles* is that they help their students remove the blocks between themselves and God. In *A Course in Miracles*, Jesus periodically indicates that this is its purpose. Although this is an ongoing process and underlies many of the 12 steps, it is most obvious in Step 7 – "We humbly asked Him [God, as we understood Him] to remove our shortcomings."

A significant difference between the 12-step programs and *A Course in Miracles* (*ACIM*) is that all 12-step programs require regular attendance at meetings with other members in order to be effective whereas *ACIM* is a self-study course (though some students enjoy attending weekly meetings with other *ACIM* students).

Chapter 9: My spiritual life begins

Although I didn't know it at the time, I believe my spiritual life began on August 16, 1997, the day after I had my last mind altering drug or alcoholic beverage. For the six months before that I was going to quite a few 12-step meetings but I also continued my drugging and drinking. Three or four of my 11 lockups were during this six month period.

Once I did stop, I went to a lot of meetings and started to acquire many new recovering friends. During my first year in recovery, I worked the 12 steps for the first time.

After roughly two years, I was able to get my driver's license back and I purchased an old pickup truck and then an old van after the pickup died on me. Although I had very little money, I was very happy. Meanwhile, my many different legal issues were getting cleared up and I was being invited to family holiday events once again.

Chapter 10: A friend gives me a copy of *A Course in Miracles*

Around the middle of 1998 a friend of mine gave me a copy of *A Course in Miracles* and I began studying it right away, reading through the Text first. Although I didn't understand everything that was being taught, I understood quite a lot and I didn't get bogged down with those parts which weren't clear to me. I think I completed reading the 669 page Text in 2 or 3 months. I'm quite certain that I understood Jesus was the author of this book at some point during this first reading.

After completing the Text, I started on the Workbook for Students with its 365 lessons. Jesus points out that we students should not do more than one lesson per day: "Do not undertake to do more than one set of exercises a day." (W-Intro.2:6) However, I initially thought I had a better idea. Since I took some of my sleep at night and took a nap during the afternoon, I logically concluded that I could treat each 24-hour period as 2 days: the first began when I woke up in the morning and the second when I woke up in the afternoon. Thus, so I thought, I could do 2 lessons each day and complete the 365 lessons in 6 months rather than 12. Here's what happened with my approach – After about 45 days of doing the lessons (I was up to about Lesson 90), I found that I wasn't really benefitting from these exercises and so I simply set *A Course in Miracles* down. It was about 2 or 3 months after this, around January of 1999, that I thought I should start the lessons again, beginning with Lesson 1, but only do one a day. From that point on, the study of *A Course in Miracles* has become "a way of life" for me.

Chapter 11: I move to Florida

By January, 2001, I had saved a little money and decided to drive down to Florida for a vacation. To get out of the snow and cold of Buffalo to the warmth of Florida for 3 or 4 weeks seemed like a real good idea. I didn't have much money but I had a tent and camping equipment so, once I got to Florida, I camped in a few of their very nice State campgrounds. It was a great trip! I attended many 12-step meetings where friendships develop like no other organizations I've ever been a member of and I traveled a lot throughout Southwest Florida where I spent all my vacation time.

While on that vacation to Florida, I said to myself: "Myself, where would you rather live – in Buffalo or in Florida?" And of course the obvious and instantaneous answer was "Florida!" So a couple of months later, in March or April of 2001, I was in a large rented moving van with all my earthly belongings and my van in tow on a trailer headed from Buffalo to Florida.

There were some significant adventurous times my first 5 or 6 months in Florida which I won't be getting into in this book but I can tell you "They were all good!" I ended up purchasing an old mobile home in Arcadia, Florida and moved in with the help of some new found friends in September of 2001. I would be living in my "new" home for about 2 years during which time I went to a lot of 12-step meetings, studied *A Course in Miracles* and overall I had a good time.

My neighbors who lived right next door to me, Bob and Donna, were an older couple and became my very best friends. I basically adopted them as my Mom and Dad. We had many great conversations in their home together. Although I didn't know it at the time, Bob and Donna really were questioning my sexual orientation. I was not dating anyone during this period but on a regular basis guys I knew in our 12-step program would come over to my house so I could help them with the 12 steps. So from Bob and Donna's viewpoint it appeared there was a real good chance I was gay. Years later, in 2008, when I returned with my 3rd wife and our baby, Tesha and Jimesha, Bob shared all this with me and we laughed together.

I remember that on the Super bowl Sundays of 2002, 2003 and 2004, I had a picnic and barbecue at my home with somewhere between 50 and 100 people showing up. It was great fun!

Chapter 12: I move to St. Martin in the Caribbean

Around late 2003, my child support to Debbie ended so my spendable income about doubled overnight. I had never been on a cruise before and some friends of mine were going on a cruise in the fall of 2003 and I joined them. And I thoroughly enjoyed it! I enjoyed it so much that shortly after this I went on another cruise by myself and again I had a great time. Both of these were Caribbean cruises and they both docked for a day on the Caribbean island of St. Martin, a very delightful place. For my next vacation, in early 2004, I rented an apartment on St. Martin for two weeks and flew over there, rented a car, and I really fell in love with the island. While I was there, I decided to rent a one bedroom apartment which was on a quiet part of St. Martin overlooking the Caribbean Ocean. It was beautiful and the rent was only $650 per month.

So on or around April 1, 2004, I flew over to St. Martin to live there for at least 6 months, the term of my lease. I also purchased a used car on St. Martin at a very reasonable price. Meanwhile, I rented my home out in Florida, not knowing if I would enjoy living for an extended period on a Caribbean Island.

As it turned out, I loved it. I quickly made many new friends and each day was a new adventure. I continued to study *A Course in Miracles* and attended 12-step meetings on a regular basis. During that 6-month period, I easily decided that I wanted to make St. Martin my permanent residence and purchased a beautiful 2-story house which, like my one bedroom apartment, was in a neighborhood which overlooked the Caribbean Ocean.

Around October 1, 2004, I moved from my apartment to my new house. Within no time, I realized that I needed a cleaning lady to help keep the house in some semblance of order. I ended up hiring a young lady named Tesha to work every Friday morning for about 3 hours. She was a delightful young lady and after a short time we would spend about 30 minutes just talking as friends before she started working. Basically, I insisted on this conversational time, telling her that she was getting paid by the hour whether she was cleaning or talking to me. I also told her that I was paying her $10 per hour, about twice the rate that most cleaning people were getting paid. Tesha didn't say anything to me at the time but much later she informed me that a couple of the other homeowners she worked for at the time paid her a lot more than I did.

At that time and during the next year and a half, Tesha also worked full time as a cook in a very nice dinner restaurant on St. Martin. She was a very happy person whether she was working or spending time with friends or alone with her own thoughts. In no time we became very good friends.

In January or February of 2006, I asked Tesha if she would like to go out with me and she said okay so we went and saw a movie together. A few more dates ensued and in short order I asked Tesha if she would like to marry me and she said yes! Very soon after this quick engagement, Tesha moved in with me though she continued to maintain her own apartment.

The next few months were great but also quite stressful. Tesha's family back in Guyana, South America (next to Venezuela) had some real and logical misgivings about our upcoming marriage, especially her Mom. You see at the time I was 57 years old and Tesha was only 25. In March, Tesha and I flew to Guyana so the family could "check me out" and I could also get to know them and start learning firsthand of this splendid country and its wonderful people. As I recall, I stayed for two weeks and Tesha for three weeks.

Chapter 13: Tesha and I move to Guyana and get married

Within the first month or two of our engagement, Tesha became pregnant and we were both real happy about this. This also caused us to want to get married as soon as possible. We had rationally decided that we would initially live in Guyana because Tesha did not have a visa to visit or move to the United States. So at the end of May in 2006 we moved to Guyana and moved into a very nice house we had rented in the Village of Atlantic Gardens on the East Coast of Guyana. On June 15, 2006, Tesha and I were married in a civil ceremony with a small number of Tesha's family present, including her Dad and Mom – John and Mayleen Fortune.

In August, we had a real celebration of our wedding at a small hotel near the coastline in Guyana. Well over 100 people attended, including Tesha's Aunt Jean and 3 of her children from Toronto, Canada, her Uncle Buddy and his two youngest children who came from England and her Cousin Denise who flew in from New York City. We rehearsed and performed a mock legal wedding ceremony with Tesha's Dad (John Fortune but everyone just calls him Uncle John) acting as the minister. It was great fun! We had a band and an open bar. Tesha looked beautiful and I danced as if I were John Travolta and everyone laughed at me. It was really a wonderful event. To the best of my knowledge, everyone without exception had a wonderful time.

The next four months were wonderful for both Tesha and me. We had purchased a car and got to visit many parts of Guyana and visit with many of Tesha's friends and family in different parts of this beautiful country. We often drove over to Grove, where Tesha's parents' house was and where every day was an adventure with all the comings and goings on there. They own a very large two story house in that village.

Sometimes we traveled by boat over to the little village of La Harmony, where Tesha and her 4 sisters and 2 brothers grew up. What a delightful place this little village is. The cabin like structure which the family had lived in is still there though it could use some repair now. It is right on the shore of the magnificent Demerara River which is roughly one mile across and very fast moving. In the little harbor where the old family home is, Tesha and her siblings loved to go swimming after a long day of work, school and play. When I think of Tesha's growing up, I virtually always think of one of my favorite Americans of all time, Dolly Parton. My recollection of Dolly's growing up was a whole bunch of kids and her Mom and Dad, hardworking, very little money but a tremendous amount of love and happiness.

Often, when I tell others about the Demerara River, I tell them it's about a mile across and makes our so called big rivers, such as the Mississippi and the Colorado, look like little streams. I often also mention that the Demerara is the smallest of Guyana's 3 great rivers.

Tesha's Dad, Uncle John, still manually farms about 80 acres of land behind the La Harmony house and lives there about 6 days a week. Periodically, he loads up his boat with an incredible variety of fruits and vegetables that he's grown and rows across the Demerara and loads them on to a public bus where he carries them either to the new family home in Grove or directly to the capital city of Georgetown where he sells them in the famous and incredible Stabroek Market.

For all practical purposes, La Harmony is today as it's been for the past 200 years or so. There's no electricity (though I think perhaps the schoolhouse and a few of the homeowners have solar or gas powered electric generators today) and no real transportation other than one's own feet. Up until about a year ago, the only access to La Harmony was the Demerara River. About a year ago, the government of Guyana built a road so it's now possible to drive into at least a part of La Harmony. From what we understand from friends and family in Guyana, this "modernization" has not yet adversely affected the beautiful and serene village of La Harmony.

During these first months that Tesha and I lived in Guyana, Tesha and the baby in her belly were doing well. Around July, we learned that our baby was a boy and we decided his name would be Peter, named after Jesus' famous friend and disciple. As for my part, I often if not always, kissed little Peter good night when Tesha and I were about to go to sleep. As the weeks rolled on, little Peter got more and more active of course while growing within Tesha's body. It was as if Peter were already with us outside of Tesha's body and we had no doubt everything was going very well.

On December 11, 2016 Tesha's water broke and we grabbed Tesha's hospital bag and pillows and drove to the hospital. The hospital rules were that only hospital staff were allowed in the delivery room. Meanwhile, Mayleen (Tesha's mom) and one or two others had arrived at the hospital. A relatively short while later, the doctor and one of the nurses came out and informed us that the baby was born stillborn.

I initially handled this tragic news quite well. Perhaps I was in shock but to this day I don't know if I was. I was very concerned for Tesha so that when the doctor and nurse told us that Tesha, who was heavily sedated, had not been told, I asked if I could be the one to tell her this very sad news and they allowed me to do so.

For the next few days, I got hardly any sleep and my mind kept getting more and more manic although I didn't realize it. Within 5 or 6 days, I had a major psychotic episode which I won't detail in this book. We held a funeral service for baby Peter at our house with many supporting family and friends attending and buried his little body at a cemetery in Grove (the village where Tesha's parents lived) with a very nice burial service.

By the next day, all hell broke loose in my mind and Tesha arranged a visit with a very qualified psychiatrist. I recall he gave me a shot of some medication which in short order knocked me out which allowed me to get some much needed sleep and rest for my mind. My psychotic episode was over, thank God.

However, the next 10 months or so were not easy for me because I was in a depressed state. Although I'd been in "clinically depressed" states at past times in my life where I was nearly totally immobilized, this period was not that severe. Today, I think of this as situational depression, directly linked to the loss of our little Peter.

During 2007, I took 2 or 3 trips back to Southwest Florida and stayed with my good friends, Bob and Donna, and attended many 12-step meetings while there. Although Tesha could not be with me (her U.S. Visa had not yet been approved), she was fully supportive of my trips to the U.S. I am convinced that these trips to the U.S. helped me recover more quickly from my depression.

In the spring of 2007, Tesha and I took a vacation back to St. Martin for about 3 weeks and it was very enjoyable for both of us. Even more important is that, while we were there, Tesha became pregnant again so that on November 5, 2007, little Jimesha was born with only very minor baby complications. What a joy she was, has been and continues to be! She's 9 years old now and at the top of her class in third grade. For the most part, she gets along with everyone and has many friends. You might be asking: "How did you get the name Jimesha?" Here's the answer: "Take 'Jim' plus 'Tesha' and subtract the 'T' from Tesha and the result is JIMESHA."

Meanwhile, while I was in Florida in 2007, I purchased a house, an automobile and an old motor home, so when Tesha and Jimesha arrived, we would be all set for our new life together in the good old U.S. of A.

Chapter 14: Tesha, Jimesha and I move to Florida

Finally, in January of 2008, Tesha's U.S. Permanent Resident Visa was approved. Because I was a U.S. citizen, our little Jimesha was automatically approved for a U.S. passport at the U.S. Embassy in Guyana. So at the end of January, Tesha, Baby Jimesha (about 3 months old), and I flew from Guyana to Florida to start our new life in America.

As we were driving from Miami Airport to our new home in Arcadia, Florida, I called some close friends and arranged a little party at our house. I think it was the very next day that we had a get together with about a dozen people, including Cosmo and Jodi who were little Jimesha's first set of U.S. God parents. As I knew would happen, everyone loved Tesha and Tesha loved everyone.

Five months after arriving, we left on our 4-month motor home trip. We went from Florida to California to Michigan and Canada and then back down the Atlantic Coast to Florida. Although we did many things and visited many places, what stands out to me as the best was driving the Pacific Coast Highway (Route 1) from Los Angeles up to San Francisco. I think this is probably the most scenic route in the entire United States.

We visited friends and family at many of our stops. Tesha got to meet all 4 of my siblings and many other family members - my brother in California, my youngest sister who was living in New Jersey that summer and my two sisters who live in the Buffalo, New York area. Naturally, they all fell in love with her and, of course, with little Baby Jimesha. They continue to believe that Tesha is the best thing that has ever happened to me and I, of course, must agree.

Following this wonderful trip, we continued with our very active life here in Florida. In 2009, Tesha became pregnant once again and, because of all the family support available to us in Guyana and because Guyana has a National Health Insurance program so the cost to us of having our baby there was not significant, we decided to have our new baby in Guyana.

Chapter 15: Our second major loss

On December 24, 2009 (Christmas Eve), Tesha gave birth to a little girl who we had decided to name Joy. Unfortunately, Joy's lungs were not fully developed and she had to stay in the hospital on a lung respirator and in an incubator. Over the next two months, Tesha would visit Joy nearly every day and, about 3 or 4 times a week, I would join her. I'm happy to say that our new little baby girl never seemed to be suffering and I would often tell her how she could look forward to spending time with us and her big sister, Jimesha, especially when we went to Disney World back in Florida. I must say that the doctors and nursing staff were excellent. Unfortunately, little Joy never got better.

On February 28, 2010, Tesha went with most of the family to a carnival to help earn some money for the family. Tesha's Mom (Mayleen) had purchased a couple of trampolines which the family took to carnivals and charged a small amount for children to jump up and down for 10 minutes or so. The family owned a truck which allowed them to haul the trampolines to various carnivals in different parts of Guyana. So this was one of those rare days when Tesha didn't go to the hospital to visit Joy. I did not go with the family that day but went over my friend Tappy's house and was having lunch with him and another good friend, Kingsley, when I received the phone call from the hospital telling me that little Joy had passed away.

Naturally, I shared the sad news with Tappy and Kingsley. The hospital told me we could come see Joy's body if we did so within the next few hours but then the body would be transferred elsewhere. Tappy and Kingsley joined me for this viewing.

When I arrived at the family home, only Uncle John (Tesha's Dad) and Adams, a close family friend, were there because everyone else was still at the carnival. I shared the sad news with these two men and, although they thought I should call Tesha on her cell phone, I decided to wait and tell her personally when she arrived home.

It was around midnight before the family got home. Within a few minutes, I asked Tesha into our bedroom and sat next to her on the bed and quietly told her of Joy's passing. She cried some and we held each other closely. If there was any exchange of words, I don't recall.

Within the next week, we had a funeral service for little Joy and buried her right next to her brother, Peter, in the cemetery in Grove. Not too long after this, Tesha, Jimesha and I flew back to Florida and quite quickly we settled into our busy and happy routines back home.

As I consider the loss of Joy compared to the loss of Peter for me, I appreciate and thank God for the spiritual progress I made over that three year period. When Joy passed, I was able to handle it like a mature and responsible adult. When Peter passed, I absolutely required Tesha's spiritual strength to get through our loss. When Joy passed, although Tesha did not require it, I was actually in a spiritual position to help her through our loss.

Chapter 16: Jimmy Junior arrives

The next big event in our family began during the summer of 2013 when we spent our 2 month vacation visiting Guyana. Jimesha was 5 and had finished her pre-kindergarten year and would be starting kindergarten after our vacation. Shortly after we got to Guyana, Tesha decided she wanted to have another baby. Without any hesitation I said okay but letting Tesha know that this baby would be born in the United States. Although quite costly, the United States, to the best of my knowledge, has the best health care in the world.

The result was that on March 17, 2014 (St. Patrick's Day), Tesha gave birth to Jimmy Junior and both little Jimmy and Mom had a relatively easy time of it. One thing we both appreciated early on was that, although Jimesha was and still is a very active baby and child, Jimmy is so much more active! What I often tell people is that one day Jimmy was crawling real fast all over the place and then he found out he could walk. Well by the end of that day he was running and he's never stopped running since. Our home was a wonderful happy place before little Jimmy showed up and with him now on board, it seems to me we can multiply the amount of wonderfulness and happiness by about 4. As I write this book draft, just yesterday we had a three-year old birthday party for our little Jimmy with about 25 friends sharing the happy occasion with us.

I would be very remiss if I didn't include another character who we were given about two years ago by the name of Ollie. Ollie is a dachshund dog (i.e., looks like a big hot dog) and is a wonderful addition to our family. He loves everyone and is great around all people from tiny infants to very old people of whom there are many here in Florida.

Chapter 17: Epilogue for *Course* students

If you know little or nothing about *A Course in Miracles*, I suggest you read pages 3 and 4 of this book (Part I, Chapter 1: Summary of *A Course in Miracles*). This will give you some understanding of what I have to say in this last chapter.

The preceding pages do, in fact, represent a brief autobiography of my life to date as the world defines autobiography.

I know, however, that this life I described is really a work of fiction. It never happened. I literally dreamed up this life.

My happy childhood, my first marriage and two children, my successful professional career, my descent into hell due to my drug addiction and alcoholism made worse by my bipolar mental illness, my current marriage and wonderful wife with our two wonderful young children, the many happy days we've shared together as well as the 'tragic' loss of our two babies .... It's all been just dreams and nightmares.

God created but one Son, Who Jesus also refers to as Christ in his *Course* and that has never changed. So when I'm fully awake from my dream and God takes the final step and I'm back home again in Heaven, I will fully know I am Christ. I can't be both Jimmy Laws and Christ – I am still as God created me (i.e., Christ). You, too, are also Christ, just as God created you.

Jesus puts it quite succinctly in *A Course in Miracles*: "Let me not forget myself |Jimmy Laws| is nothing, but my Self |God's one and only Child or Christ| is all." (W-358.1:7)

To reinforce this very important idea, Jesus includes the following fact in three different lessons: "I am as God created me." (title of Workbook lessons 94, 110 and 162) God created me as His only Son, Christ, and that is Who I am in truth.

It is for this reason that in the title of this book, I used the term "me" rather than "Me." Jimmy Laws, in my dream world, is of course something. However, all dreams and nightmares are, of course, not true. So, in truth, my dream world and my identity as Jimmy Laws, the hero of my dream world, never happened.

While I'm in this dream world, I'll continue to play my part and, if you decide to contact me, I will respond to the name Jimmy Laws.

Printed in Great Britain
by Amazon

10649551R00130